CHRISTIAN CIVILISATION

CHRISTIAN CIVILISATION

WITH SPECIAL REFERENCE TO INDIA

WILLIAM CUNNINGHAM, M.A.

GYAN

Published by

Gyan Publishing House
5, Ansari Road
Daryaganj, New Delhi-110002
Phone: 011-47034999, 9811692060
E-mail: books@gyanbooks.com

Distribution Network
gyanbooks.com
India, USA, Canada, UK, Australia, France

ISBN: 978-81-212-9424-9 (PB)
First Published, 1880

2nd Impression 2023

Printed at: Gyan Press, Delhi.

CHRISTIAN CIVILISATION

AUTHOR: WILLIAM CUNNINGHAM

CHRISTIAN CIVILISATION

CHRISTIAN CIVILISATION

WITH SPECIAL REFERENCE TO INDIA

BY

WILLIAM CUNNINGHAM, M.A.

London:

MACMILLAN AND CO.

1880.

PREFACE.

THOUGH the following chapters were not all written at the same time, or with the same object, they form parts of one train of thought, since they describe the nature of Christian Civilisation, and discuss the best methods for its maintenance and diffusion.

In treating of Catholic Experience, Christian Morality, and Christian Policy, I have embodied the substance of three sermons, two of which were preached before the University of Cambridge.

The few pages on Church Organisation may serve as a brief response to the Bishop of Colombo's appeal—at the S. P. G. Conference in 1878—for an investigation of the past in the hope of obtaining light for the difficulties of the present. No one can be more fully convinced than myself how valueless, in regard to all questions of details of administration, the results of such research may be. Even if the lesson of the past were clearer than it is, there would still be need of practical wisdom to determine how far it can be applied in the changed circumstances of modern days. It is, therefore, with considerable diffidence that I conform to the conditions attached to the Maitland prize, and publish, as the three last chapters of this book, an Essay which, in urging the entire severance, for administrative purposes, of Native and European Christians, advocates a view that seems to meet with little approval from those who are practically conversant with the subject of which it treats.[1]

W. C.

EASTER, 1880.

[1] The Organisation of a Native Indian Church, with special reference to (*a*) local requirements, (*b*) the existence in India of various forms of Western Christianity, and (*c*) the importance of Church Unity.

CONTENTS.

NOTES.

I.

CATHOLIC EXPERIENCE AND INDIVIDUAL OPINION.

ONE of the most praiseworthy characteristics of our age is its real earnestness in seeking for the foundations of a creed. Men have come face to face with deep problems of existence. There is but little jesting as they ask the world-old question, What is Truth? and wait in weary suspense, only too fearful of any bias that may induce them to be satisfied with an imperfect answer. There has probably never been a time when so many men have been forced, in their fear of error, to remain in this attitude of suspense, careless of the unrest in their hearts, the chilling of their sympathies, and the deadening of their energies. To them it seems that the avoidance of error is the furthest step they can take in the pursuit of truth: nor need we deem their earnest search less admirable because it is so hopeless. Theirs is a sad suspense who, seeking for a faith, are yet forced to doubt whether man can attain to any religious truth at all.

We may, however, remember for our comfort that while men are still debating how experience is possible, a body of positive knowledge of the external world has somehow grown up. If we contrast the accurate knowledge which the ordinary Englishman possesses of his relations to the material world with the vague impressions of the Kafir or the Bushman, we note a wonderful advance. There has been for countless generations a constant storing of human experiences of the material world, a constant reflecting upon them, and a co-ordinating of new discoveries. Of all this store of positive knowledge we are the heirs; and most of our days of study are occupied, not so much with seeking new discoveries, or even with verifying past ones, as with seeking to appropriate the results of the accumulated and co-ordinated experience of the race in regard to the material world.

When we consider how slowly this body of knowledge has grown, and that a large proportion of the race has scarcely shared in it at all, we cannot be surprised that there is so little agreement in regard to the more difficult questions as to man's relations to the Intelligence that rules the world. As to the existence of such an Intelligence we do not care to argue; because we are well aware that, like the principle of the uniformity of nature, it cannot be proved to the Understanding without a *petitio principii.* But we are not amusing ourselves with metaphysics, and are content to assume the possibility of experience and the existence of a God. These transcendent questions we waive: and taking for granted that a God exists, we ask whether we can hope to learn not only that He is, but what He is, and thus obtain some positive knowledge as to His relations to us.

Whether there be any such religious knowledge or not, we can at least guess at the conditions which would be favourable for its growth. It has been during the last few centuries, when each has been free to pursue his own researches to his own satisfaction, that the experience of the human race has been most quickly amplified and co-ordinated, and thus that the knowledge of the physical world has advanced most rapidly. There were times when it was feared that if the corrective influence of authority were removed, men would fall into and promulgate strange errors about the material universe. And even though these fears were proved not wholly groundless, we may yet feel that —not to mention the positive gain under the new system—foolish fancies were more quickly refuted by the investigations of new observers than they could have been by an authoritative tribunal. And we believe that it is just the same with regard to religious truth; that, too, may emerge more clearly if the craving for individual conviction obtains free play, and external pressure is withdrawn.

To some this may seem a dangerous doctrine. It may perhaps reassure them if we turn to a precisely parallel case, and consider the manner in which Christian morality grew up. It is difficult for us at this distance of time to realise the nature of the struggle which took place in the minds of many religious men during the first century. They had been brought up in the strict acceptance of the code that had been given at Sinai, a code which defined their duties to God and man; and they feared that if the slightest infraction of this code were permitted, there would be no unimpeached authority to maintain the commonest duties of morality. Some there were who thought that while each Christian man sought to live the life of Christ, there would be a greater safeguard for morality than in the dictates of an impracticable code. At first appearances were against them: there were strange individual vagaries and shocking crimes in some churches; but at length, in spite of shame over individual sinners and backsliders, the mind of the Church was made up, a common Christian Consciousness of what was right and what was wrong came to assert itself more widely, more forcibly, than had ever been done by the Jewish Law. Some made their liberty a cloak for licence, but it was under this régime of liberty that the Christian Consciousness of morality[1] was formed. It was in no indifference to morality, but in a firm faith in the power of the indwelling Christ, that St. Paul could say of any duty,[2] *Let every man be fully persuaded in his own mind;* and it is in no indifference to the creeds of the Catholic Church, but in a firm faith in the abiding presence of God's Holy Spirit, that we may look out on the world of doubt and discussion around us and say, *Let every man be fully persuaded in his own mind.*

For as in the sphere of action my conscientious conviction is the supreme rule for me, so, too, in the sphere of thought, each man's conscientious belief is, even when mistaken, supreme for him: to his formed subjective conviction let him above all be true; let his honest belief be sacred to others.

[1] Similar remarks might be made about worship. While the Jewish sacrifices were discarded, and their Sabbaths no longer kept, the Christian Consciousness came to enjoin the celebration of better worship, and the keeping of the weekly and yearly festivals of the resurrection, even in spite of the vagaries of individuals who forsook the assembling of themselves together.

[2] See Note, p. 139, on 'S. Paul and Moral Indifferentism.'

Never can the cause of truth be served by cowardly dissembling, never by the cruel coercion of the consciences of our fellow-men. It is terrible when we learn that those whom we love and honour have, albeit in reverent obedience to what they believed was true, discarded historic Christianity and cut themselves off from the noblest fellowship of faithful men; but though we may long that their convictions should change, we cannot wish that they should for a moment be untrue to the *full persuasion of their own minds.*

It might have been unnecessary to dwell thus at length on *liberty of conscience*, if it were not desirable to contrast it with the curious claim that is occasionally put forward to a *right of private judgment in matters of religion.* There may be some who mean by this no more than the liberty which has already been described, but the phrase frequently betokens some unwarrantable assumptions and strange conclusions. For there can be little doubt that the phrase, as commonly used, implies indifference to religion : those who maintain that every man,—

the careless scoffer, the earnest student, the diligent philanthropist,—has each a right to his own opinion, must surely think that religion is a thing of little moment, where right and wrong are not of any great importance. We never hear men protesting in favour of a right to maintain crude conceptions in matters of science; and if each man is to be supported in his claims to maintain his own personal prejudice in matters religious, on the mere ground that 'though a poor thing 'tis his own,' that must be because we are wholly careless about the subject.

Or, perhaps, because we are wholly sceptical. We may have come in spurious humility to believe that God and His nature transcend our powers of apprehension; that, do what we will, we never can understand aught about Him; that He is for ever unknowable: then assuredly is one vain figment of the imagination as good as another; then, but only then, has every man a right to his own opinion in matters of religion.

For those of us who are not indifferent, who believe that the knowledge of God is the highest human good—since therein standeth our eternal life,—and those of us who are not sceptical—since we believe that they who do His will shall know of His doctrine,—such at least will claim no right to maintain their own opinions; it is not of a right they will talk, but of a duty: they will account it the duty of every man to search for the knowledge of God; the duty of every man to seek it eagerly and unrestingly, to strive for a fuller and fuller understanding of the mind of God, of His will for each and for all, till at length the earnest seeker shall find, and shall come to know even as he is known.

In truth the so-called right of private judgment is like all other rights, strictly correlative to the duty of private judgment; just in so far as any man has fulfilled his duty in seeking for the knowledge of God, just in so far has he a right to maintain the opinion he has formed. There is surely no other sphere of human thought in which this principle is not readily admitted. When any one makes a statement on any disputed point in science or criticism, and adds, 'That's my opinion,' do we not instinctively inquire as to the speaker's right to have an opinion? Do we not consider how far he has fulfilled the *duty* of careful investigation? Only in so far as earnest study has led to full persuasion do we treat his opinion as something that deserves respect at our hands. Well would it be, if, instead of proclaiming an abstract right to think what we like about God, we would each ask ourselves, How far has my patient seeking God's truth, how far has my earnest doing of God's will, given me a right to my own opinion of Him?

While, then, we most fully recognise the sanctity of each man's conscientious convictions as a guide for his own conduct at each particular time, as something his neighbour dare not impugn, we may yet repudiate the scepticism or indifference which would put each and every religious opinion on the same level. They are of very different degrees of worth, and command very different degrees of intellectual respect, according as the grounds on which they are formed are good or bad. If I demand attention to any opinion, or respect for any teaching, it must be not merely because it is my own conscientious conviction, and I am fully persuaded in my own mind, but because of the grounds on which my opinion has been formed. There is no question before us now as to the manner in which any religious opinion has been presented to the mind, but simply as to the logical value of the arguments or evidence on which it rests. The central belief of Christianity—that God is reconciling the world to Himself—may have appealed to different minds in different ways: some men have adopted this conviction through the influence of early education, others by later study, others by what they would describe as a sudden intuition; but with these varieties of circumstances or temperament we have nothing to do. It is for us to consider the grounds of religious belief as a power in the world, not the history of its formation in this or that individual mind. Thus to discuss the various grounds on which religious opinions are based, will be to enable us each to judge most truly of the worth of our opinions—not merely of their sanctity for each one of us, but of their objective value and real truth.

It seems that there are two main classes of evidence on which our religious opinions may be rested: either on *reflections drawn from observed or reported facts* in the external world, or on *direct religious experience.* Of each of these sorts of evidence we may endeavour to estimate the value.

Very many and interesting arguments in regard to God and His ends in creating the world, or His modes of governing it, have been framed from a consideration of the course of nature. Time after time, as men have looked on the sun that rules by day or the stars that shine by night, they have repeated that the *Heavens declare the glory of God;* and truly this voice has gone into all lands. Nowhere among men has God left Himself without a witness in that He *gave them fruitful seasons, filling their hearts with food and gladness.* Men have risen from the thought of the bounty of nature or the might of nature to dwell on the goodness of an Almighty God. Yet though this witness is *true,* it is faint and imperfect, and capable of misinterpretation; it ever gives an uncertain sound. Hence the sorrow we feel when we know of those who, as they eagerly scan the phenomena of nature, yet refuse to view them as the vesture of the invisible God. We may compare, too, the testimony of the holy men of old who asked, *Canst thou by searching find out God?* or who declared that the *world by wisdom knew not God.* Helpful as reflection on *observed* facts may be to many minds, it is yet but a poor basis for a structure of religious doctrine. Matters of faith cannot rest on the evidence of sense-perception, or on disputed interpretations of the facts of nature.

Recorded facts may give us fuller evidence regarding the character of God, but not a firmer foundation of our religious belief. Some have delighted to trace the path of God in history, have seen His justice in the rise and fall of nations, His goodness in the gradual ennobling of the human race. Yet are there not many who, as they read of these struggles, find no trace of a guiding hand or of a controlling purpose? And even when we turn to that page in the history of humanity which reveals to us most clearly the character of God—when we study the reported facts of the life of our Lord, full and clear as their teaching is, we must yet remember how variously they have been interpreted by those who have accepted the accuracy of the reports. That reflection on these facts does not compel our assent to one true system of religious doctrine, is only too clearly shown by the history of the heresies of the past as well as by the schisms of the present day. *Spiritual things must be spiritually discerned.* The life of our Lord gave the most perfect presentation of eternal truth which was possible in the spheres of space and time, but the truth was revealed through Him ; He did not pretend to give a demonstration which should force conviction on unwilling minds. Valuable as the Bible stories may be for the confirmation of our faith, they do not in themselves furnish a firm footing on which to found our religious doctrines. For it is ever *faith that is the evidence of things not seen*, and the human Understanding is not convinced by these observed or reported facts, of the truth of any religious opinion. If my religious system has no better support than the reflections of my Understanding on what I have seen or heard, it is built on a worthless foundation, and has no claim to the respect of others, even though I be bound to be loyal to it in my conduct.

Well is it, since the reflections of our Understanding are so little trustworthy, that we can turn to another source, and rely for truth about God on *direct religious experience*, —a direct religious experience which each of us may enjoy for himself. Now, as of old, the grace of God that bringeth salvation is manifested abroad; to-day as ever do the Spirit and the Bride bid us come; this very day we may each listen to the Psalmist's invitation to *taste and see that the Lord is good.* Nor are these the mere metaphors of fervid poetry. There are thousands in this land to-day who know in their own souls the blessedness of the man to whom the Lord imputeth not his sin; there are thousands who have been sustained when they cast their burden on the Lord; thousands who have received the strength of Christ in the Holy Communion; and those who have thus tasted the power of the world to come, tested by their personal experience the present aid of the eternal God, have a sure ground of cónfidence which needs no subtle sophistry to sustain it, and cannot suffer from the attacks of a more subtle reasoning still.

It is sometimes the fashion to decry such direct religious experience as mere emotion, the outcome of a heated imagination, which will not stand the cool criticism of a clear Understanding. It was thus that S. Paul was taunted by the Judaisers of his time ; they said that the vision, which had been so real to him, was but a fleeting unsubstantial fiction of his imagination. It was not only in his lifetime that his conviction was scouted, for works written long after his death contain a full measure of scorn for the profession he put forth. Yet S. Paul's own conviction was unshaken ; *he had not believed in vain.* The vision was no fleeting impression; it had been the starting-point of a power within his soul which had led him through countless trials in the service of his Lord. The permanence of his conviction, its continued effectiveness in his conduct, were sufficient proofs that God was indeed working within him, and that he had truly been taught of God, not deceived by his own fervid fancies. Such religious experience may reach us through what we call our emotions rather than through what we term our intellect; but it need not be the less, on that account, a source of objective truth. The persistence of the sense of God's presence and the effectiveness of this faith, through a long course of years, are the best possible evidence that it is no figment of our own imagination, no passing sentiment, but a true experience of the present help of the eternal God. And they who have thus come to know God Himself—who commune with Him—have indeed a sure, an unassailable ground for their religious opinion; others may discuss the arguments *pro* and *con.*, and reason and reflect, but to them it is given to *know*, for the Spirit beareth witness with their spirits.

Yet if such personal experience gives the greatest possible intensity of conviction, we may yet notice that it does not insure any immunity from error. As there were cases of wild individual licence while Christian morality was growing, and of strange vagaries of practice while Christian worship was taking an orderly form, so have there been strange eccentricities of pious opinion. There is need for something that may serve as a corrective for private fancies, and that test is to be found in the religious experience of other men. Fellowship in the earnest devotion of God's people, fellowship in the pious deeds of faithful men, is a noble incentive to good, and a noble corrective for religious egoism. Nor is it only from our contemporaries that we can learn these lessons. The knowledge of God to which the saints of old attained has not perished as they passed away. Ever and anon have their experiences been treasured for our learning. Their confession of sin, their joy in forgiveness, their adoration, their aspiration,—all the deepest contrition of the psalmists, all the noblest enthusiasm of the prophets, have been stored for us; they testified that which they *knew*,—their own religious experience, the things to which their souls were moved by the Holy Ghost, that is the testimony of the holy men of old.

There is in these writings a great store of human religious experience. We shall perhaps value it more truly when we remember how frequently these testimonies have been indorsed; when we remember that the words of a psalm were the fitting vehicle for the thoughts of our Lord in His last agony; when we remember how the Consciousness of the Church slowly sifted out these writings that gained the witness of God's Spirit in Christian hearts, we may see what a weight of religious experience confirms the testimony of the writers of the Old and New Testament: there is a Catholic experience which declares to us the deepest knowledge of God to which men have attained.

Ever as the ages have rolled on, and individual souls have through divine aid attained to a clearer vision of God, they have put forth some truth which Catholic experience has taken up and confirmed. Our Lord has revealed the way to the Father, and thousands who have trod in that way bear witness that they do indeed come to the Father by Him. The apostles proclaimed the presence of God's Spirit striving with men, and thousands have known His strengthening influence and purifying power. And as for the faith in the Eternal Trinity, so for all other points of Christian truth or devout practice we may urge the evidence of those who have themselves known God, who are abiding in Christ, who are reconciled to the Father, who are led by the Spirit of Truth. Such conviction as this cannot be assailed. No external evidence, no *à priori* guessing about God, can stand beside Catholic *experience* OF God.[1]

And thus it is that we look to Christ's Church on earth as *the pillar and ground of the truth.* In the received writings of the Church we have a store of the deepest religious experience of human beings; in the creeds of the Church we have the formulated utterance of what God's people in all ages have felt, and therefore known of Him. A religious heritage has been treasured at the cost of countless lives, its truth has been tested by myriad minds, preserved by the Church, proclaimed by the Church, which,

[1] See Note, p. 144, on 'Catholic Experience and Common Sense.'

just because it preserves and proclaims Catholic experience of God, is the pillar and ground of the truth.

Here then in the Catholic faith, defined in the creeds, set forth in Christian teaching, shown forth in Christian worship, we have positive religious knowledge—the accumulated store of human experience of God. Some there may be, some there must be, who have never thus known God's present power, nor tasted His goodness, nor known the blessedness of the pardoned. Let them beware how they dare, therefore, to deny the reality of such religious experience. It is this personal knowledge of God which has given the greatest impulse to human beings to purify themselves even as He is pure ; it is this personal religious experience which has been the most powerful factor in the reformation of the world. Nor can we point to any influence which has been so persistent or so effective—which has proved itself so real—as the co-ordinated human experience of God which is treasured in His Church.

But if we dare not scorn this heritage of religious experience, we need not impotently bow before it as an authority whose search has been exhaustive, and whose results we cannot verify for ourselves. May we not hope that as the ages roll on, God will reveal yet fuller knowledge of Himself to the prophet minds, who may draw from the Divine treasure things new as well as things old? Must we not each long, as we hear of the beatific vision which other eyes have seen, that we too may be thus fully persuaded in our own minds? For the truths which our fathers have learned may be sought by us too, and may be found. The path lies plain before us. Those who do His will shall know His doctrine; those who seek shall find. For God will indeed give His Holy Spirit to them that ask Him,—a Spirit which shall show to them too the deep things of God, so that walking in His holy ways, tasting of a peace which the world cannot give, rejoicing in a hope which none can destroy, they shall live the life which is hid with Christ in God, and thus be *fully persuaded in their own minds.*

II.

CHRISTIAN MORALITY AND PRIVATE INTEREST.

WHILE there is so much doubt about the Christian creed, we need not be surprised at the frequent questionings as to the value of Christian morality. Some regard it as defective, in its apparent neglect of the more masculine virtues; some even profess to have discovered purer and more excellent teaching in the doctrines of Buddhism. Undoubtedly, however, the most frequent ground for criticism is to be found in the marked differences between the principles of Christian morality and the lives of the members of Christ's Church. If the letter of the precepts of the gospels is sometimes inapplicable to the free citizens of a modern realm, it cannot be denied that too little effort is made to apply their spirit to the circumstances of our present life.

Though this fact may lead men to doubt the reality of much Christian profession, or even to question the effectiveness of religious belief as a motive to conduct, it should be remembered that others than Christians have failed to realise their ideal of life. Such failures do not concern us at present, for they do not impugn the excellence of the Christian morality nor diminish the value of the service which the Church has rendered to the world in constantly maintaining an unattained, but not therefore unattainable, ideal of human conduct. For when S. Paul wrote, *None of us liveth to himself*, he was depicting an ideal, not stating a fact. There never has been a time in human history when the mass of men in the world have ceased to aim at being their own masters and doing what they like. Even of the Church just planted by the apostles it could be said in bitterness of spirit, *All seek their own, not the things of Jesus Christ.* Yet none the less do these words express, in short compass, the aim which the Christian must seek to realise, the standard by which he must try himself, as it is the measure by which he shall be judged at last. None of us—members of Christ—is his own servant, to fulfil his own personal wishes or seek his own personal gratification. We dare not do what we will with that we call our own, since we are not our own but bought with a price. We have another Master for whom we are bound to live, and to do His service is the supreme rule for our conduct here,—a rule which is supreme and all-embracing. No moment of the slave's time is his own ; nor is there any direction in which his master's will fails to constrain him ; and there is no side of human action, no moment of his allotted life, in which the Christian dare claim to live for himself, forgetful, neglectful, regardless of the Master he serves.

Truly this is a hard saying. We need not be surprised that none can fully realise this ideal in their life, or that many are offended by it. It is surely a sad thing, however, when this ideal of human life is not only left unattained but boldly repudiated,—when influential teachers proclaim an exactly contrary doctrine, and popular opinion accepts the pleasing delusion, that it is well for the world that each man should seek to serve his own interests, and that general welfare will follow if only every man will live for himself.

Even though it has been recently discredited by many authoritative writers, there would be no difficulty in quoting from popular authors' works many passages where this unchristian teaching is explicitly set forth; but to do so would not enable us to measure the extent to which it is implicitly maintained. It is quite impossible to converse on social questions in ordinary company without finding it usually assumed that in all temporal matters it is certainly the right, if not entirely the duty, of every man to do the best he can for himself, working for himself, in his own way, for his own reward. And any one who, in the face of the unchristian practice of our work-a-day life, dares to maintain the Christian ideal, must bear that stigma of sentimentalism which rests on those who believe that the truth of God is a greater power than the wisdom of the world.

It may indeed be maintained that our existing régime, where each has perfect freedom to pursue his own advantage, where the motive of personal gain and getting on in the world is the sole ground of appeal in favour of honest labour or diligence in business—that this régime has called forth most marvellous results. In every direction of trade or manufacture the progress made has been truly wonderful. Whatever test of material prosperity we may choose to take, be it the development of our own resources, be it our relations with our neighbours, be it the accumulation of our wealth, the progress has been rapid in the extreme. The free play for the exercise of self-interested energy has brought a vast accretion of gain; the consideration of private advantage has served as an effective stimulus to the carrying out of great undertakings: surely then it may seem that an influence which has been thus effective in increasing the material wealth of the nation has conferred a very real benefit, and that *results* have justified the plan of every man living to himself.

But while we fully recognise the great gain

which has arisen from the rivalry of keen competition, gain from the increasing severity of the struggle of each to hold his own against the rest, we cannot ignore the positive loss that is entailed, as we see how the keen strain of competition calls forth a *disregard for others* and a *disregard for right.* It may surely be maintained that our greater store of goods and chattels is a dear bargain, if it has been purchased at the expense of encouraging a harsher tyranny towards the weak, and of lowering the current tone of morality in regard to commercial dealings.

A careful study would only confirm the impression that these charges are wholly justified. Free competition gives a great opportunity for the strong, but it crushes the weak; it is inherent in the very nature of competition that the weak cannot hold their own against the strong—that the poor cannot hold their own against the rich; and thus, year by year, while one vast fortune after another has been realised, the squalor and misery of the masses in our towns, and the wretchedness of the labourers in the country have continued. If these men have profited at all, which may fairly be doubted, they have profited to an infinitely less extent than the wealthy; relatively to the rich men of the day, the poor are worse off than in the ages when steam was unused. And if any particular case of scandalous oppression is brought to light among tailors, among sempstresses, among children in factories, we are ever told that no individual employers are responsible for these things, but that it is forced upon them by the 'exigencies of a keen competition.'

Not less true is it that in the effort to undersell a neighbour many a great house has stooped to positive dishonesty. The cotton cloth which Lancashire sends to India is shamelessly adulterated; the rails which have gone from our ironworks to America or the Continent have been too often useless for any continued wear and tear. And these two staple industries are but examples of what goes on in every department of work, in local trades, like building, as much as in the giant industries of factory districts; and again, the same excuse is urged, that the times are out of joint, that the dishonesty is not chargeable to individual men, but is forced upon them by competition.

As we thus see ourselves in a society where the severance of class from class is daily becoming more marked, where the benefits of increasing wealth are daily becoming more monopolised, where the struggle for existence entails a lowered moral tone and an overwhelming temptation to fraud, can we find much cause for self-gratulation in considering how much our shipping has increased during the last century, or how much paper has passed from hand to hand in the clearing-house? May we not ask ourselves in all earnestness whether the free play of self-interest has justified itself by its results, or whether we might not hope for a nobler national life if we set before ourselves a wholly different ideal, and worked for the coming of a time when no man should live to himself? This at least we may say: Those who have any qualms as to the excellence of the civilisation which we are diffusing by chicanery and slaughter over the habitable globe,—those who have no faith in the unrestrained self-seeking of each as efficacious for the good of all, may perhaps do well to consider the real meaning of the moral principle which was affirmed by S. Paul, and which has been confirmed by Catholic Christian experience, *None of us liveth to himself.* Nor is this unnecessary when we remember how much Christian teaching on this point has been exaggerated, and therefore caricatured.

In bygone days when the world was less leavened by Christian teaching and habits than it is to-day, there were men who despaired of it altogether, who came to believe that the world which God had made very good, the creation which Christ is redeeming, was utterly corrupt; that all contact with it would bring defilement; that all exercise of natural human activities was likely to lead to sin. Some there were who forsook the daily distractions of secular life for the quiet contemplation of the cloister; some who sought in the depths of their own souls for a mystic communion with God; but all of them were inclined to condemn the exercise of natural activities as if it were a yielding to the corrupt inclinations of unregenerate man. How far this exaggeration was forced upon them by the miserable iniquity of the evil world which was present to them then, we need not inquire; nor does it concern us to ask how far they could find apparent sanction for their conduct in the precepts of our Lord, or in the example of His earthly life. It will suffice to say that the ideal of many earnest men in these dark days was one of *self-repression*,—of the repression of healthy desires and noble ambitions; that their discipline and training were directed to the utter abnegation of self, so that all might be alike moulded after the image which they had figured in their minds, of the one great model for all Christian and all human aspiration.

But that is not the doctrine which S. Paul preached. It may have been a needful discipline in days gone by, when the superfluity of wanton self-indulgence could be most manifestly opposed by an exaggerated form of self-denial: none the less was it an exaggeration. We are called, not to repress our powers, but to use our powers for God; it is not by *self-repression*, by destroying our inborn dispositions or acquired faculties, that we can best glorify God, but by *self-dedication*,—by presenting to Him our souls and our bodies, yielding all that we possess to Him, yearning to use it in His service. If we are bidden to cease to live to ourselves, that is not because our life is to be less earnest or active, but because its earnestness and its force is to be directed to another and a nobler end. The figure of a slave, which S. Paul has kept before his mind, may be a helpful illustration here; the powers which have been yielded to the mere pleasing of self must not be repressed, but rather be dedicated to the service of our Master.

Nor need we forget that there is much service to be done for God here; there are those who are ever speaking of life here as a preparation for the service of God hereafter; but there is no other possible preparation for a higher life of God-serving beyond the grave than an active life of God-serving here and now. We cannot fit ourselves for the work God is preparing for us by dreaming about it; there is a reward hereafter, but it is given to those who labour and struggle here. The Christian life of self-dedication need be no life of withdrawal from the intense realities of earth and its struggles; it is assuredly pursued by those who, in obedience to the Divine command, go forth to their daily toil, and subdue the earth; it is fulfilled by those who, living in the world, are not of it, and thus undertake every task in the name of the Lord Jesus. And those who thus understand and thus adopt the Christian ideal will not be slow to rejoice in every new phase of human industry, in every step of material progress, in every new victory of human skill, in the free opportunities for the development of the powers of every man. One mechanical contrivance after another has been introduced which may serve, rather than has served, to lighten the load of human drudgery,—which may leave a little breathing space for each to become a nobler being, and therefore a fitter subject for self-dedication to God. Each new channel through which commerce flows may aid in the communication of higher and lower human races, and may become, rather than has become, the means of ennobling

The energy which goes forth throughout the realm of nature, and subdues it to the use of man,—the patience which waits for the harvest, and plans for the pursuit of vast undertakings,—these are great human powers, which may do a great work for God, and therefore for man. It is not of the results of this progress we complain, but of the evils which have accompanied it, and which have accompanied it so largely, because that progress has been so often stimulated by a miserable motive of self-seeking and self-pleasing, not by the high desire of doing whatever our hand finds to do with our might, because it is God's will for us. We may all join in rejoicing at the rapid development of human industry, though we cannot laud the self-seeking which has so largely stimulated it.

Thus it is that we need have no fear lest in adopting this exalted Christian ideal any present earthly good should be thanklessly ignored, or any material gift of God carelessly neglected. Private self-interest is not the sole motive that can stimulate to the development of the resources of our earth; for indeed when we take a wider view of industrial progress in this isle, we can recognise an aim that has played a more powerful part. We call to mind the little bands who settled among barbarous tribes, to toil on barren isles or dreary hills—for the glory of God ; we call to mind the Cambridge thegns who gathered nine centuries ago, and bound themselves by a solemn pledge to seek peace and ensue it—for the glory of God ; we call to mind the solemn councils, where men denounced the horrors of baronial war and proclaimed a solemn truce—for the glory of God ; we call to mind the craftsmen who combined to aid each other here and hereafter, and to do their work to the glory of God ; and we say that the foundations of our industry were laid, not by those who were seeking their own gain, but by those who were not living to themselves, but dedicating their deeds to God. And as it was founded so has it grown. Not in mere self-seeking, not in total forgetfulness of God have the noblest of our discoverers toiled ; not wholly self-regarding have those philanthropists been who protested against manorial thraldom, who overthrew the tyranny of planters abroad, and who struggle—not perhaps always wisely—against the worse tyranny of competition at home. In so far as freedom for individual self-development has grown, it has grown because in every age there have been men who have been consciously labouring for their Father in heaven, or perhaps unconsciously working for Him when they were devoting themselves with their whole souls to the least of His children here.

That Christian ideal which has floated before so many minds may still be our aim. We do not crave for the continuance of a ruinous and bitter rivalry, where estrangements ever become wider and wider, and where the weaker ever go to the wall. We look for a true social organism, in which every man shall find his place, and every man shall fill it; where there shall be the greatest scope for the development of the powers of each, and the most harmonious working of the powers of all. But this we cannot have if each is striving to outdo his fellow: only when each of us shall have truly dedicated himself to God,—only when each shall seek not for the pay he would like, but for the place for which God has fitted him, and in earnest devotion to God shall do his duty in that state of life in which he shall have been placed.

There may be many who admit the beauty of this ideal, who feel that in a society so constituted we should miss the class jealousies and blatant oppressions of our own day; but those who plume themselves on being practical men may perhaps be satisfied to dismiss the conception as Utopian. But the Christian scheme of life is not Utopian,—not so Utopian as the fanciful plans of which we sometimes hear for creating an artificial harmony between opposed self-interests, by complicated schemes of partnership, or for blinding men as to the direction where their self-interest[1] points by offering a bonus on their labour. It involves no psychological miracle, and is not impracticable for men as they may be in a busy world. In the Utopias which theorists have tried to create, they have given exclusive prominence to some one motive; they have constructed a New Har-

[1] See Note, p. 146, on 'The Interests of Capital and Labour.'

mony on the supposed devotion of each to the good of all his comrades or designed *phalanstères* where the pleasures of industry should constrain each man to do his share in the necessary round of labour: this is as much a one-sided view of life as that of the medieval saints who excluded all human secular interests from their rule of devout life. But Christianity as we know it is not one-sided; it includes and consecrates all secular interests; it harmonises all human springs of action. The love of God need not be set forth, cannot truly be set forth, as the sole impulse to action. It is far more than this,—it is the supreme end to which all natural impulses may be directed. Each natural instinct or passion or desire is hallowed when it is regulated by conscious reference to this highest end. The instinct of self-preservation in the struggle for existence may be hallowed by the hope of preserving one's self to serve God better; the desire of accumulation may be hallowed by the thought of providing for those whom God has given to our care, and so through all the round of appetites and desires and passions: they will work in some way; they cannot be extinguished, but they may be directed so as to subserve the chief end of man; or they may be misdirected, undirected, uncontrolled by those who seek to live for themselves alone, and who awake at last to feel all forms of dissipation insipid, or to know the blank misery of having lost all love for God and all sympathy for man in their hasting to be rich.

If mere personal impulses, appetites, and passions and desires may be directed to the highest end, we may take more courage when we recall the existence of those social affections and nobler deeds which present a problem to the devotee of self-seeking, but which take a prominent place in the Christian scheme of life. Throughout the length and breadth of this land there are innumerable streams of charity, not always well directed; there are splendid triumphs of care for others among the very lowest outcasts on our streets: there are elements of unselfish regard for duty in quarters where it is least expected and never recognised.[1]

[1] As, for example, in the splendid unselfishness of many Trades Unionists, who submit to terrible privation for no personal benefit but to maintain the status of their class.

All this diffused duteous feeling would work a wondrous reformation if it were organised; and it can be most truly, most permanently organised, when all men shall come to labour for that one sole end which is common to all alike—the glory of Him who made them.

Thus it is that we believe the Christian ideal is one that may be realised—no unattainable Utopia, but a practicable scheme of life; nor need we despair of men being aroused to toil for this highest end, or of their being helped to continue true to this noblest aim. We may, indeed, confess with shame how the miserable spirit of self-seeking has eaten into the core of our whole being, and even tainted our religious life. There are so many among us who look for their private blessedness as the end of their hopes, their private attainments as the aim of their struggle,—men who, in their highest aspirations, *seek only their own, not the things which are Jesus Christ's.* And if the seeking of our own interests has thus marred our holiest rites, we need not wonder that it has so mastered our social institutions. To think only of one's own aims and gains is so easy, so natural, such a strong stimulus to active exertion; the glory of God is so far above us that it seems very hard to bring that thought to bear on the trivialities of daily life, or to raise our souls to such a level that we shall do everything in the name of the Lord Jesus. Hard indeed it is, and therefore let us lift up our eyes to the hills from whence cometh our help,—help to keep ever before us the Christian ideal of life, grace to check our petty self-seeking, and to live in loyal service to our Master. For the same power which has preserved an unattained but not unattainable ideal in the Church, will bring the feeble desires of our hearts to good effect. Still are men strengthened by His might in the inner man; for we believe in the Holy Ghost, the Lord and giver of life, who is ever extending the Church to embrace all human interests, as well as all human tribes; who is purifying the Church to become more worthy of her Lord, till at length there shall be—for other eyes than ours to see—a kingdom of God on an earth where *no man liveth to himself.*

III.

CHRISTIAN POLICY AND MODERN STATECRAFT.

In contrasting Christian morality with the current egoism, we have had much occasion to use that phrase, *The glory of God*—a phrase on which it seems all the more necessary to dwell because it is specially characteristic of Christianity. Only when we go forth to declare a perfect reconciliation between God and man can we point to the glory of God as the truest aim for the energies of man. It is this that has been forgotten by those to whom the words have been a stumbling-block. They have seemed to think that God was ever in antagonism to His creatures, and that His glory could only be obtained at the expense of His creatures; just as human self-glorification is gained by triumphing over others. But God is not glorified by triumphing *over* His creatures, but by triumphing *through* them; *in Him all live and move and have their being*, and therefore in His triumph all have their share. When the earth is most fully replenished with all good things,—when its resources are most fully developed, most wisely garnered,—when the dumb creation shall taste less of the brutality of man, and yet subserve more truly its own functions in the realm of nature, then will men repeat of the actual earth what God said of it at first. As all becomes very good and creation ceases to travail, God the Creator is indeed glorified; but not less truly does the well-being of man coincide with the glory of God the Father.

And so, too, while we assert that the true end of Christ's life and death was that *He might be Lord of the living*, we may yet remember how He himself declared that the kingdom of heaven is within, and that there is no antagonism here between the master and the slave: the more entirely each man is enslaved to Him and He is glorified by human devoted loyalty, the more may each one of us come to know a perfect freedom. In submitting to Him as our master, in following Him as our leader, we shall be indeed glorifying God the Son, but we are not less truly attaining to the highest type of manly virtue.

So, too, if, as we trace the gradual purifying of gross hearts, the raising of degraded peoples, the taming of savage manners that has marked the course of history, we worship the Divine Spirit that is ever striving with man, and feel that this redounds to His glory,—we are not less truly rejoicing in the progress of those *in* whom He strives,—we are not unmindful of the ennobling of Humanity. Each phase of the Divine glory which is manifested in time is also a new and a noble blessing for mankind.

Thus it is that those who hold fast to the Catholic faith, who believe that in Christ man is reconciled to God, that by God's Spirit man is purified, even as He is pure,—they at least will feel that there is no true human longing, no manly ideal, no high aspiration which is not included in their thought when they acknowledge the glory of the Eternal Trinity, and set this before them as the one worthy object of human endeavour.

This aim gives the clue to all maxims of Christian morality in all personal relations of life. In all duties to one's-self or to one's neighbour it may serve as a sufficient touchstone of right and wrong; but we are often tempted to think that the principles which regulate the petty affairs of daily life, and the ideals which are the noblest for personal adoption, are inapplicable, if tried on a large scale. They are said not to hold good for the relation of a State to each of the citizens who, sprung from it, have been nurtured in it; and to be still less applicable to the relations of one State with another. Yet how dare we pretend that we are seeking to make Christ the Lord of the living if the most important relations of men to each other are to be regulated without conscious reference to the glory of God? We cannot understand the full scope of the Pauline teaching unless we are prepared to recognise that there may be not only Christian morality, but Christian policy.

In insisting on the truth that Christianity holds out a political ideal, we need not descend to the arena where burning questions are canvassed by rival candidates for popular favour. Genuine party differences have arisen between men who could not agree as to the means of realising a very similar ideal ; grave evils have arisen as each party in turn has been tempted to seek its own aggrandisement rather than to maintain its ideal. We are not concerned with the failure of any men to carry out the ideal they cherished, but with the nature of the true political end ; and we believe that the only worthy aim for the politician is just precisely that which is paramount for the individual man,—that *Christ may be Lord of the living*—that everywhere and in everything *God may be glorified.*

There are, of course, many who would at once reject this belief. Macchiavelli popularised the doctrine which hypocrites, who repudiate his teaching with their lips, adopt in their hearts, that political expediency may override all other considerations, and that we must be satisfied with a low standard of rectitude and truth and honesty in those affairs which are of the highest importance to living men and to their posterity. But those who acknowledge the glory of the Eternal Trinity as the supreme end of national as of individual life, will not dare to labour for that end by unhallowed means, or to admit that any unrighteous political expediency can work directly for the glory of God.

Some there are, too, who split human life into separate spheres, who speak of the State as concerned with civil affairs and secular life, but regard it as indifferent to religion altogether; and they would assuredly deny that a religious aspiration afforded the truest political aim. Some in half-despair, and some in open defiance, have fallen from our faith; and thus in this so-called Christian land there are too few who cherish the Christian ideal as the guiding principle of our national life. All the more necessary is it that we should inquire more closely into the nature of Christian policy.

1. In considering the question of Christian morality, we found that it allowed free play for the harmonious development and exercise of all human powers; in looking more closely at the Christian end of action, we have just seen that it embraced all possible human aspirations, while it ennobled them. And so, too, in matters of State, all the particular objects which men set before themselves as the outcome of their policy, are embraced in the Christian aim; all other good things are implied for those who are seeking the glory of God.

One such end of wise Government is the development of the material resources of the realm. We read in the history of days gone by of one great ruler who was specially successful in this endeavour. His fleets visited distant lands; his capital was an emporium for the trade of all the surrounding countries. Yet the enterprise and business capacity by which Solomon enriched Jerusalem were subservient to a higher end; the greatness and wealth of the king were witnesses of the goodness of the God he served; thus it was that the heathen queen, seeing the wealth and power of that realm, was led to glorify God as she said, '*Blessed be the Lord thy God, which delighteth in thee, to set thee on the throne of Israel: because the Lord loved Israel for ever, therefore made he thee king, to do judgment and justice.*' And as in that day, so in ours; a Government which increases the material prosperity of a nation is adopting one means for advancing the glory of God.

There was another characteristic of a good government which was not so clearly seen in Solomon's time—the well-being of the citizens—internal happiness. The dream of a blessed time when each should sit under his own vine and his own fig-tree seemed deferred; the tiller of the soil groaned under fiscal oppression, which resulted in a rebellion against the heir to the throne. Had this blot been removed, had the tribes been happy under that rule, it might have lasted for long; and thus lasting, how effectively would it have set forth the glory of God. The empire of Solomon may serve as a warning by its failure, as well as an example by its brilliance. Any measures which promote the security and happiness and contentment and well-being of the people are means to setting forth the glory of God.

And that other object for which politicians strive—influence abroad—that too may set forth the glory of God. When we think how largely this idea enters into the prophetic conception of the Messiah's kingdom, when we remember how greatly, as a matter of fact, the cause of civilisation among backward races has been furthered by the pressure put forth by distant potentates, we cannot forget that this object of policy may be a means to advance the glory of God.

Thus we might go the round of all the particular objects for which wise rulers strive, and show how they are all included in that one great aim; all these things are but means to one great end. Only a wealthy nation, only a happy nation, only a powerful nation, can clearly show forth to the world the glory of God.

2. As a first characteristic of Christian policy, then, we may say that it does not neglect any of the objects for which wise rulers have striven; and we may add that

while it does not neglect any, so it does not *overvalue* any, but sets each in its true place. It does not, like Solomon, seek for wealth at the expense of internal well-being, or, like Louis Quatorze, sacrifice domestic resources to ambitious display in foreign circles. Each of these different and conflicting objects is kept in its true place, because each is regarded as a means to the final end of all human life; none of these objects is looked upon as an end-in-itself.

It needs but a slight acquaintance with the history of Christian nations to let us see how often they have fallen short of this noble completeness, and by adopting narrow and one-sided views, have sacrificed the whole national life to one particular idol.

In our own history one instance lies on the surface. There have ever been men who have regarded the development of our commercial and industrial resources as the supreme end of our policy, and who have led us into countless miseries in consequence. At the times when Charles II. submitted to any indignity at foreign hands, so long as he extended the area of our trade; when stock-jobbers bribed their way into power which they used for their own ends; when a sister kingdom and our Colonies were harassed and impoverished for the sake of English capitalists, we were surely pursuing wealth as an end-in-itself. And to England, too, the love of money has been the root of all evil. If that spirit be not dead among us, if it still shows itself in our treatment of our noblest dependency, we may yet be thankful that the national mind is awakening to the wickedness of that folly. Those who are most keenly interested in the growth of our trade have spoken unanimously through their representatives, and have declared that they care for no extension of commerce which brings a blight to distant or to savage peoples. The working-men, at least, of England have learned that the increase of the national wealth is not to be pursued as an end-in-itself.[1]

Other political objects may be sought for in the same narrow spirit. The physical well-being of the citizens may be pursued as an end-in-itself, not as a means to a higher

[1] See Reports of Trades Union Congress, 17th Sept. 1879.

end. None of us need underrate the blessings of good health. All of us may welcome the efforts which are made to improve the sanitary conditions of English homes in town and country; but even if cleanliness be next to godliness, it is not godliness; and though health is a glorious blessing, it is neither the chief end of man to preserve his health, nor that of a nation to promote its diffusion. And when we see throughout the greater part, if not the whole, of Christendom a system of legislation which aims at the promotion of mere health, careless of civil freedom, and defiant of morality itself, we need not pause to ask whether it is successful in its petty object or not, before we condemn it as careless of the glory of God.

Against this one-sided pursuit of things which are good as means to an end, but unworthy of being followed as ends themselves, there is but one safeguard. Only when we cherish a high ideal of what man is, of the place he may fill in the world, —only when we keep before us an exalted view of what a State may be, can we truly judge of the worth of these objects which men pursue. It is when we raise ourselves above the greedy national desires of the present for wealth or for health or for influence,—when we see from a lofty eminence the far-reaching results of the unrestrained indulgence of these national desires, that we can be warned of our danger, and seek to limit our desires by subordinating them to a noble end. And shall we not best and most truly understand these things if we can enter into the mind of God,—if we can come to understand His purpose, the view which He takes of human life here? Nor is that hidden from our eyes. He has revealed it to us; He has called us to work for an end which includes our highest hopes and aspirations for ourselves; He has set before us the glory of God as the true aim of human life. Nor is it merely through the lips of prophets that God's thought for us has been revealed. We may see it as the controlling motive of the one perfect human life; we may well embrace for ourselves, and for our country, that aim which inspired the Christ *who both lived, and died, and revived, that He might be Lord of the living.*

If it be true that the conflicting objects of policy can only be thus reconciled, that the State can only be guided by a far-seeing policy, when men cherish a high ideal; if it be true that the highest and truest of all political ideals is given us by entering into the mind of God and seeking to know His will, what is this but the old assertion that the State rests upon religion, and that its progress depends upon religion? What other influence is there to raise men's minds above the peddling expediencies and greedy desires of the present? What other help to raise their aspirations and to keep them constant to their truest aim? And thus as we look for means by which a more glorious future may be opened up for our country, we can but turn to the accumulated religious experience of Christian men, to their apprehension of God's mind for us, and therein find our ideal; we can but turn each for ourselves to those means of grace by which men have entered into closer communion with God, and come forth with strength to live for Him. Therefore we believe that as in days gone by, so now, and so in time to come, will Christ's

Holy Catholic Church give the ground of our political hopes and the source of our political progress.

But here we must distinguish. Thus to maintain the necessity of the Church's influence for the progress of the State is not to insist on the perpetuation of any one form by which the Church exercises her influence. The Divine wisdom is still to be found in her inherited experience, Divine strength in her communion; yet as the ages roll away there come to be new channels through which her voice is heard: the old order changeth, giving place to new, but God is still making His will known, still giving His strength to those who seek Him. Nor need we fear that our national progress will succumb to the attacks of an advancing Secularism, if we have faith in that God who is present with His Church on earth, and who is, through that body of faithful men, working in the world.

There were days when the power of the Church on earth was wielded by the Bishop of Rome; when no other influence but his could make itself felt in the tumults of the time to uphold a Christian ideal or give a

Christian direction to the activities of that day: and when at length the personal authority of that potentate was broken in this land, there were good men and true who saw no hope for their country, no other means by which the claims of righteousness and godly fear could gain a hold upon capricious tyrants. For the maintenance of that old order Sir Thomas More and Bishop Fisher suffered a glorious martyrdom. Yet while the Roman supremacy was passing for ever, God was purifying the English Church to become a truer, a more faithful witness in this land; and now as one by one the adventitious aids by which men have bolstered up the influence of the Church in this land are dropping off, we may perhaps awake to realise the truth that what were once meant as supports have survived as barriers; and that with a growing life and deepening earnestness, the Church can exercise a potent influence on the destinies of the nation through the conscientious convictions and earnest work of her faithful children. Those who believe in the Divine foundation of Christ's Church, those who believe in the Divine presence within it, will not fear that any change in its civil status can destroy its spiritual power.

It is ever a relief when pressed with the distresses of the present to recall the triumphs of the past; to look back to the overwhelming difficulties which attended the first planting of the faith. The religious problem of apostolic times was a hard one, and one that was of the first importance for all future ages, for as the young shoot was then directed so has the tree grown. It was indeed hard to detect the true standpoint for the Church to take between the requirements of the Jewish Law in which she had been schooled, and the needs of the heathen world to which she was commissioned. Distracted by the fear of forsaking God's law, men were yet to find a fuller guidance in the teaching of that Spirit who could work a full persuasion in their own minds. Fearful of discarding a definite code, they yet found a true canon for morality in seeking to live not for themselves, but for their Master. While the hopes of a Jewish empire were failing, they were yet taught to strive for a nobler realm, when Christ should be Lord both of the dead and the living. And He who guided the Church in her first great struggle will be with her working in a wider sphere—wider, because just as the Church has grown, so has it come in contact with a greater range of human misery and sin, over a wider area of the world, in more complicated social systems. As science and criticism extend, the conflict of individual opinion becomes more confused; there is more need than ever for a voice to maintain Catholic experience of God. As the misery of our masses increases, and the dealings of men with each other get more reckless, there is a deeper need to proclaim the highest principle of morality. As our political power comes to touch more distant nations, or to deal with more minute details, while it is diffused amongst larger numbers, there is more need to maintain the highest political aim. There is indeed a great task before those who are commissioned to meet the vagaries of individual opinion with Catholic faith, to oppose the licence of individual self-seeking by Christian morality, to pursue amid the anarchy of individual interests the end that our Lord set before

Himself in His work. Truly the task is great; but we need not therefore quail before it, we dare not therefore relinquish it. Rather let us go forth in the strength of Him who is with us alway even unto the end of the world. God's Holy Spirit has worked in all ages, forming the Catholic experience of God, maintaining the Christian canon of conduct, and setting forth the highest end of human life. In all sides of that Christian Consciousness we may be partakers through that good Spirit, so that, fully persuaded in our own minds, we may each live, not to himself alone, but in loyal devotion to the Lord of the living.

IV.

THE UNITY OF THE CHURCH.

WE have been thus far considering the work which lies before the Church in facing the powers by which it is opposed. There must almost necessarily be some little repetition as we come to consider the nature of the Church as an active institution. We shall, however, be looking at the matter in a new aspect while we dwell on the internal life of that body, which we have hitherto viewed in relation to its assailants.

There are two different aspects in which Christianity may be considered: we may lay special stress on its work in the individual heart, and try to delineate the power which it possesses of purifying the life; or we may view it in its influence on the world as a power which has to do, not principally with the inner consciousness of individuals, but with the regeneration of society. Both sides of religious life must be kept in view in all Christian effort. The strong desire for the personal salvation of individuals with whom men have come in contact has often been the strongest incentive to religious zeal, and those who are bearing the burden and heat of the day may often be unable to hope that their feeble work can have any influence beyond the circle of their immediate hearers. For us who view the matter in its broader aspects, the case is different. It is not so much the immediate progress of the Gospel in touching human hearts as its ultimate success in regenerating society that we have to consider.

We cannot help recalling, too, that this is the aspect of the progress of the truth that comes out most prominently in the reported teaching of our Lord. We do not seem to find Him dwelling so much on the personal religious experience of His followers and the blessedness of their lot, as on the growth of His kingdom in the world. The slow but sure progress of the society that He founded is ever in His view, and even in those parting words where His personal union with His disciples is most strongly depicted, He urges this on them as a means of bearing much fruit. We shall enter most closely into the mind of our Lord if we think of missionary effort as really directed at regenerating society, and at the conversion of individuals not as the end of our labours, but merely as the enlisting of more labourers into the real work of the Church. As we read the reports of labour abroad, and the accounts of baptisms, we are sometimes apt to forget that that rite is but the initiation into a path of Christian life and work, not in itself the end to be aimed at.

We should be inclined to say, then, that the object of Christian missions is not to save individuals only, but rather to spread the kingdom of God; to enrol new citizens by baptism, and to organise these citizens in one great army that shall do their best in the service of their King. When once we grasp this view of the subject, we are struck with the infinite importance of all questions of Church organisation. They really mean,

How shall God's army be best disciplined so as to do its work most effectively?

The point we have attained gives us a clear view of the relation of the Church as a whole to her members. We can think of the Church as a great institution stretching far into the past, which ever embraces new members, but which consists not merely of the congregation living in one place, not only of the whole number of living members, but of the living and the dead bound together in one holy fellowship; the living are the heirs of the faith and experience and triumphs of the dead. New members are being constantly embraced, who thus become partakers in the treasures of religious faith that have been preserved by the Church—partakers in her treasures, and partakers in the duty of freely spreading to others the blessedness which has been freely bestowed on themselves. So far as organisation goes, their task is that of modifying the methods approved by the experience of the past so as to suit the exigencies of the present.

Those who start from the thought of Christianity as addressing itself to individual souls, and finding its end in their conversion, will be apt to take another view of the nature of a church, and to consider it as a congregation of individuals who meet together for mutual edification and exhortation to the doing of common duties. The members compose the church; it is nothing but the aggregate of the members. The faith of the members is the faith of the church, and the members at any one time are fully competent, by describing the faith that is in them, to define the creed of the church, or to make such arrangements for its organisation as shall seem to be most suitable for their own needs.

According to the one view, the Church is the world-wide everlasting kingdom of God, which possesses in her Scriptures and creeds and rites and prayers a noble religious heritage. It may be that none of the members in some towns or districts attain to her ideal of devotion, or to a full realisation of her faith. It is offered to them, they may come to attain to it; but the truth to which the Church witnesses is a greater and nobler thing than the opinions of her actual living members in any one place. The Church embraces the members, but does not consist only of them; she always maintains a nobler witness than can be given by the frail human beings who partake of the privileges she affords. According to the other view, the church consists of a body of men with really faithful hearts, living together, and in full Christian sympathy with one another.

From these two different conceptions of a church, or the Church, follow two different ideas of Church unity. Those who believe in one kingdom of God upon earth, will mean by Church unity a oneness of all Christian men, in all places and at all times. They will cherish a sense of sympathy with the saints of old, and with God's people throughout the world; they will fear to discard ruthlessly anything that proved helpful to the men of days gone by; they will piously cherish the memory of their spiritual ancestry, and fear to break away from the living chain that binds them to the first founders of the kingdom. To break away wholly from the past is to pronounce a condemnation on our fathers in Christ, and to break the unity of the Church. Those, on the other hand, who think of a church as consisting of the living members, will mean by the unity of the church the full sympathy of these members with each other. They will care little for the religious experience of the past so long as they have full religious fellowship in the present.

We have thus seen how, from giving special importance to one or other of these two different aspects of religion, men are led to form very different conceptions of the nature of Church life, and consequently of Church organisation. We can easily see how either conception, if exaggerated, might tempt men into serious error; how some may attach undue importance to the external worship of the Church, and the place of those who conduct it, till the necessity of inner participation by the members is almost forgotten. On the other hand, we may have men so wrapt up in satisfaction at the completeness of their mutual Christian sympathy, that they are unable to look beyond their own narrow groove; and, all unconscious of fellowship with primitive or medieval Christianity, they have no scruple in condemning doctrines and practices which they have never attempted to understand. If the Western Church of the fifteenth century, or the Eastern Church of earlier (or later) times is a standing warning against the one error, the other attitude of mind was surely present in some members of various sects at the time of the Protectorate.

We dare not neglect either side of religious life; fully convinced of the necessity of personal faith, and keenly alive to the value of present religious sympathy, we dare not discard the truth that there is a kingdom of God planted in the world—a visible Church which, begun in apostolic times, has continued and flourished ever since. Guided by one Spirit, and holding to one faith, the army of God is assuredly one: the members are joined to one Head, they have one hope, one aspiration, and if Christ be not divided, that visible Church, which is His body, is truly one. Indeed, we believe that it is only by cherishing the heritage of religious experience that has been treasured in the one Catholic Church, that we can secure a high ideal of devotion at which individuals may aim, and a true basis for the fullest sympathy between individual men. In missionary labour at home or abroad men are bringing new members within the pale of the one Church, where they find the noblest type of devotion for their own souls, and feel the fullest fellowship with their comrades.

To this whole view of Christian life and advance there is an objection that immediately arises. It is said, What do you mean by the one Church? There are many bodies of Christians, each of which claims to be the true followers of Christ; which of these is the one Church that is to be extended? and is the work of all the rest to be condemned, because, even though they cast out the spirits of evil, they follow not with your particular body of Christians? These are very grave difficulties, which do not disappear until they are faced, and till we ask more earnestly than we have yet done, What do we mean by the unity of the Church? We answer that it is a unity of the Spirit, which has never been perfectly expressed by identity in the doctrine and practice and organisation of the Church throughout the world, but which we hold to as an ideal that we are striving to realise. To ask which of these various bodies is the one Church, is to ask a question that cannot be answered, for it is to ask which of these various parts is the whole; but we can ask—I. How far has this ideal ever been realised? II. How can the unity of Spirit be preserved amid outward differences? III. How far are any set of men striving after the maintenance of this unity of Spirit? By attempting to examine this article of our faith, and to trace their relation to this principle of the unity of the Spirit, we shall best understand the relation which various bodies of faithful men bear to each other.

I. How far has this idea ever been realised? The most cursory glance over the field of ecclesiastical history must convince us at once that there has never yet been any actual society which at all approached to the ideal of unity. We need not look for it after the great schism between East and West: Arianism, Novatianism, and Marcionism carry us back till little later than the time of the successors of the apostles; and thus we find a rivalry between different organised bodies, each of which claimed to be the one true Christian Society. If we do not find such patent schism in still earlier times, this was chiefly because Christianity was but little organised, and so the parties could not range themselves readily in antagonism to each other. We cannot say that the spirit of dissension was absent when we remember the bitter opposition that was encountered by S. Paul himself: the existence of disputes in regard to doctrine is abundantly witnessed in the Epistles. Very various standards of Christian conduct were also current in different, and even in the same communities; the method of governing the Gentile churches was not identical with that which held good at Jerusalem. If there was no schism in the first century, there was every possible dispute in regard to doctrine and practice and discipline.

But even if, as we thus look backward, we find no evidence of this unity having ever actually existed on the earth, in any adequate manner, we need not at once conclude that it is an unattainable, impracticable ideal; we should have more ground for fearing that, if we could say that unity was a blessing which had been once enjoyed by the Christian Church, but one that it had failed to preserve. For if we try to view the progress of the Church from the beginning onwards, we shall find not a little evidence of a gradual consolidation of Christian experience in regard to many matters, and a consequent progress towards agreement and eventual unity. Of the first century we have already spoken, of the Judaisers, of semi-heathen philosophers, of worse than heathen sinners, of disorderly assemblies, of unruliness and jealousy in every congregation. Terrible as may be our half-heartedness, unseemly and scandalous as are our janglings, the shortcomings of our Church are not those of apostolic times; on each of the great controversies that distracted that time, the minds of Christian men are made up, and in its relation to these matters the Church is at one.

Let us take, first of all, these discussions which embittered the path of S. Paul. The relation between the Jewish and New Testament Dispensations is no longer a matter in dispute. We have no controversy now as to the continual obligation of the Jewish Law, or next to none; for even though there be much difference of opinion in regard to the force of the Fourth Commandment, Sabbatarianism has not come forward as a separate sect in recent times; there is difference of opinion, but it is comparatively slight; there is no open schism, and as regards the relation of Judaism to Christianity, the Church is at one. Turning to the other controversies of the apostolic age, we find that they too are set at rest. Speculative difficulties about the nature of God and God's relation to man are no longer a cause of schism, not because they have been settled in such a way as to remove the difficulties which the human understanding feels in contemplating them, but because hundreds and thousands of Christian men and women have tasted and found that God is good. The religious experience of centuries may fairly be set against any speculative prejudication, and this religious experience is formulated for us in the creeds of the Church. And this being so, we may fairly say that on all fundamentals of the faith the Church is really at one. In east and west, in all the branches of the Catholic Church, and among all evangelical dissenters, the Apostles' Creed and the Creed of Constantinople are accepted. There are few who claim to be called Christians, none who would not be more accurately described as theists, who openly abjure any part of this one faith.

This is also true of the sacred writings which are received. Even if there is little agreement among critics as to the date and authorship of many of the books of the Bible, there is a practical unanimity about the limits of the Canon. In England and Scotland there is a wide difference of opinion about the use to be made of non-canonical writings, and this was an element of discord in Puritan times. There are minor differences in the various versions of the original tongues, and in the readings of that text, but these are of little moment. For all practical purposes of Christian life there is but one Bible.

So far there is real agreement among all professing Christians, but even the most bitter controversies give evidence of common ground. It is often said that the parties which are most nearly at one are apt to be most bitter in their antagonisms to one another, and the very fact that there is a discussion shows that there is something or other in which the different parties agree; and we believe that the discussions which have so often existed as to the best form of Church government—Episcopalian or Presbyterian, Independent or Connexional—do testify to an overwhelming consensus of opinion that the Church must be governed in some way, and cannot continue if it is unprovided with officers and leaders. We doubt if this was so generally admitted in Corinth, not to mention other Churches in the first century.

Another bitter controversy testifies to another point on which there is a general unanimity. Amid all the discussions of the relations of Church and State, one thing stands out: there is a general agreement among Christians that religion ought to be a powerful influence in political matters; the difference is as to the form in which this influence should make itself felt. Some say the head of the Church should rule over all kings; some would have a close harmony between the religious and political administration in each country; others would rely on the religious instincts of individual citizens; but all these various parties agree that political duties are to be done in a religious spirit. This is a practical belief of the very highest importance; it is one that was hardly held in the times of pagan Rome, or even under the Christian emperors of the East. There have been men who have rebelled against it, and who have held that the world was so evil that the true duty of a Christian man lay in holding aloof from all the concerns and interests of secular life; but specious as this opinion is, the experience of Christian men throughout the world has unmistakably pronounced against it.

There are other points on which a similar consensus might be noted. We might show how in the present day, in our own land, all parties make appeal to the inner convictions of their hearers. An Anglican is what he is, a Roman what he is, a Baptist what he is, because he believes that the form in which he holds the truths of Christianity is the most satisfactory to the unprejudiced inquirer after truth. They are at one in regard to the court to which they profess to make appeal. Enough has, however, been said to show that if the unity of the Church has always been a matter of faith and not a thing of sight, there is yet a progress towards unity, inasmuch as there is a constant consolidation of Christian experience.

II. Yet the personal problem remains for each of us. Each of us must belong to some branch of the Church, or some sect of Christians. Between these branches—not to mention the sects—there are considerable differences of opinion and cultus. How far amid these differences may a sense of the unity be maintained? How far this may be accomplished we cannot say; but there is no difficulty in showing how it is to be attempted—*by a reverent regard for Christian experience.* So long as we are endeavouring to enter into and understand the religious experience of Christian men in all ages, so long as a sense of fellowship is thus preserved, so long are we keeping the unity of the Spirit. There may be wide differences of opinion, wide difference in religious habits and devotion, but so long as we are able to enter into their struggles, and take them as warnings or encouragements, so long are we truly at one with them.

There is, perhaps, some danger of a misunderstanding here: some there may be who would contend that all that has been hallowed by the use of ages, that has continued as a valuable habit among many religious men, has sufficiently justified itself, and becomes binding upon all. This is never so; the final decision of what is right for me rests with me; my conviction can never be overridden. Not less true is it, however, that in forming a conviction, I may do so on insufficient grounds, and leave out of sight a large mass of valuable evidence which lies to my hand; if I limit my view to my own individual experience, my decision cannot be of such value as it would if I also take into account the Christian experience of the past as well. So long as I am consciously using the Christian experience of all ages as a help to my own life, so long am I maintaining the unity of the Spirit.

An illustration may be found in the recent controversy which was raised in the House of Lords in regard to the confession of sin to a priest. I may never have felt the need of so doing, and may be inclined to condemn the practice as wholly unnecessary, and, since it is sometimes abused, as one to be utterly condemned. On the other hand, I may take into account the religious experience of the good men in many ages, who have found the value of the habit—of such men, to name only Protestants, as Luther,[1] Cranmer, Latimer, and Ridley,—and I shall then feel that if this new evidence makes no difference in regard to my conviction as to what is right for me, it throws a different light on the habit itself, and alters my opinion of those who practise and encourage it. Those who are seeking to take into account the experience of Christian men in all ages, are showing themselves careful to preserve and zealous to advance the unity of the Church.

[1] E. B. Pusey, *Advice to those who exercise the Ministry of Reconciliation, etc.* xxv.-xliii.

A reverent regard for the Christian experience of the past will also serve as a means of understanding one another now. Each of the various Christian sects existing in England to-day has had its origin within a recent period; if we understand the circumstances in which they arose, we shall be best able to comprehend the real nature of the position they take; it thus affords a means of escaping from the personal embitterments of our own years, and dispassionately considering the meaning and results of two different principles.

While we have admitted that the unanimous voice of the past can never be authoritative for the individual conscience, we yet contend that those doctrines and practices which have come more and more to commend themselves to Christian minds, are not likely to be cast aside in time to come. By reverently reviewing the Christian experience of past ages, we are likely to have a firm hold on those principles which have come to be beyond the region of discussion; we are likely, too, to be on the right side in regard to questions which, if not yet set at rest, are gradually approaching that condition. This habit of mind will insure a firm hold on those Christian truths which are most thoroughly proved, since they have the largest measure of religious experience in their favour; it will also insure the greatest sympathy with the saints of old, and the clearest understanding of the views of opponents now. It is thus that, in spite of outward differences, the real unity of the Church may be most effectually preserved.

III. There is no other way than this in which unity may be maintained. People are always going about saying that Christians ought to lay aside the minor differences and unite in the great essentials of Christianity; but this is mere idle clap-trap, unless some test be given which shall decide what is essential and what is a minor matter. The loudest cry of this sort arose in England in the seventeenth century. Laud[1] demanded a union on fundamentals, and a laying aside of minor differences; so did the Puritans:[2] but Laud meant a union in Catholic worship

[1] Sermon on Ps. cxxii. I.
[2] *Life of Sir John Eliot*, ii. 119.

and a disregard of theoretical theology; the Puritans meant a unity in regard to theoretical theological principles, and divergence of practice in regard to worship. And the principle we have stated enables us to give a meaning to the empty formula: fundamentals are those things which have found favour with Christian men most universally; non-essentials are all on which the mind of the Church has never been made up.

This, then, is a basis on which Christian unity may be attained, and none other has ever been suggested; it is next desirable that we should consider how far various Christian sects are prepared to meet upon this ground. We have already alluded to a class who cannot be expected to do so; those who believe that each congregation is a self-dependent church cannot consistently look beyond that congregation for needed help and guidance. In so far as they believe in one universal Church, they believe only that true Christians are found here and there in all communions, and that, could these true Christians be separated from the rest, we should have a true Church; inasmuch, however, as they are only known to God alone, the true Church on earth is invisible. In thus thinking of scattered individuals as forming, unknown to themselves, an invisible Church, they sacrifice all that is inspiring in the thought of Christian fellowship. It is not only an invisible Church, but a Church with no conscious life; such an invisible Church is not an ideal that men are striving to realise, and so long as men do not recognise the one Catholic Church as something worth striving for, we can have little hope of their being willing to learn from the experience of other Christians, or to sacrifice any jot or tittle of their own opinions. Independents and Baptists who do not believe in one Church, cannot be expected to promote the unity of the Church.

Wholly different is the character of Presbyterianism. It aims wholly and distinctly at the establishment of a cosmopolitan Christian community, of which each Christian nation shall be a member. In its halcyon-days in Scotland, Presbyterianism claims to have embraced the whole nation in its system;

and it is always to a reconstruction of the old Scotch Church on a different basis that the most earnestly religious men look forward. They hold to the ideal firmly enough, but it may be doubted whether they are alive to the best means of realising that ideal, for their view is limited to a definite period of Christian life which they regard as the model for all time. It is not necessary to dispute as to the character of Apostolic Church arrangements—though even on this historical question the Presbyterian position requires little refutation—till we have answered the question, Why should the organisation of a scattered half-Jewish sect at the time of the Jerusalem Council be taken as a model for the Church for all time? Why should the experience of all subsequent ages be ignored? Presbyterianism, by its definite appeal to one short period, is opposed to that catholicity of Spirit which is the essential condition of Christian unity.

Whatever objections may be urged against Methodism, it does not lie open to the criticisms which have been made on Independency or Presbyterianism. It too has a full recognition of a Christian community as an ideal, and makes the very fullest use of Christian fellowship as a help in leading a Christian life. Nor does it adhere rigidly to one model of government. Within the last few years many changes have been introduced, and its whole economy has been remodelled; in fact, the power of Methodism lies to a great extent in the practical instinct which enables it to adapt itself to current needs. The danger to which such a society as this lies open is that of being too easily influenced by passing opinions and popular movements. There may be a danger of want of stability where there is so little regard to the tradition of the past, and so much care for the needs of the present; but there is nothing in this Methodist system as there is seen to be in the Independent, or in Presbyterianism, which is in itself inconsistent with catholicity of Spirit.

Of the various branches of the Catholic Church it is unnecessary to speak. While the sects do not take *catholicity* as a watchword, the Greek, Latin, and Anglican communions do. It was important in regard to the former that we should see how far they contained elements that would link them with the great body of Christian life, from which they seemed to have cut themselves off. Where, however, as in the case of the great branches of the Catholic Church, there is a definite historic continuity, and they are obviously inheritors of the treasured experience of the past as preserved in the creeds, the canons, and the services, we need not pause to consider the differences of detail that exist between them.[1]

We are thus obtaining a clearer idea of the best means for invigorating or introducing a Christian civilisation through the growth of the one Catholic Church ; we have seen what is meant by the unity of that Church, and how it may be most truly maintained ; and we have considered how far various bodies of professing Christians may be expected to co-operate in the regenerating of society by extending the Church. The success of Independents or Baptists in bringing individuals to a knowledge of the truth need

[1] Compare, however, especially in its Indian bearing, Father O'Niel's *Contribution to the cause of Christian unity.*

not be underrated because we say that there seems to be scarcely any link by means of which they can be united in co-operation with other Christians for the extension of Christ's kingdom. This is far less true of Presbyterians and Methodists. They cherish a noble ideal, if they differ from the great majority of Christians as to the way in which that ideal may be realised, and as to the best system for organising God's army in the world. To these questions of greater detail we must now turn.

V.

CHURCH ORGANISATION.

I. *Various Forms of Government.*

SO far our investigations have shown us that the system of organisation which is supported by the greatest body of Christian experience, which is, in fact, catholic in its character, is more likely than any other to serve as a common ground for various bodies of professing Christians. We must first ask, What system has thus most chiefly met with the approval of Christian men?

In order to decide this question, we need not enter on the difficult discussion as to the nature of the original organisation of the Christian Church.[1] It will suffice to

[1] I may content myself with stating an opinion that it was much like the existing Jewish system. The (Christian) Synagogue in each town was under the supreme direction of a (Christian) Sanhedrim, at the head of which was James the Just. I have discussed this at length in *The Churches of Asia*, §§ 7, 17, 25-27.

point out that before the end of the second century it had passed away, and been replaced by something else. The Church organisation of the first century was unworkable, and the Christian Consciousness decided against it; so that there is a *primâ facie* case against the success of any system that claims to be a simple reproduction of arrangements whose failure has been proved.

The simplest way of approaching the subject is by looking at the needs of the community and considering the various duties, for discharging which officers were required. There are three different clerical duties which we commonly distinguish: one man is spoken of as a good parish worker, another as a capital organiser, another as a powerful preacher; the duties of visiting, of ruling, and of teaching are all different in their character, and require different talents for their due discharge. Perhaps of these the duty of teaching is on the whole the most important, or at least was the most important before the printing-press came to play such an important part in the life of the people; but those of the personal superintendence of the flock, and of using the alms, and administering the discipline, and directing the energies of the community, are also of the very highest importance. The sense of the Church has on the whole been in favour of separating these three offices: the deacon is called principally to the pastoral visitation of the people; the presbyter principally to the duty of teaching; and the bishop principally to that of ruling. We do not, of course, suppose that their efforts are to be limited to these special duties; the bishop, as a presbyter, often preaches; the presbyter rules in his own parish; but the difference of these functions has been a *raison d'être* for the specialising of these three offices.

We can find ample confirmation for the advantages of this threefold division of Christian labour in communities where one at least of these names is a cause of offence. Presbyterianism, as delineated by John Knox, or as maintained by Richard Baxter, recognised these three offices: the pastoral visitation was largely committed to the elders, the ministers were to preach, and superintendents were to play an important part in ruling; and even in the present day, when superintendents are ignored, it is true that the office is practically filled by those ministers who, as effective speakers in the Assemblies, come to be so much occupied with Church business as to require the aid of colleagues for the work of preaching.

A similar practical, though not nominal, recognition of three functions in the Church is found among Wesleyans. The class system provides for the discharge of one, and provides effectively, so far as the earnest members are concerned, if it gives little room for the effective supervision of the half-hearted; while the duties of ruling are discharged by those selected to be members of the Conference: the threefold division is implied here also, if not explicitly recognised.

No further discussion of the duties of deacons and presbyters is required; it is worth while, however, to consider the functions of ruling and administration more carefully, and to see what is implied in them in those cases where they have been committed to individuals consecrated for this particular purpose. The bishop's rule is never a personal one: he always appears as the mere instrument of carrying out the discipline that has been ordained by other powers. In the earliest ages we find the bishops describing themselves as the mouthpiece of the Church where they presided; and if, in later times, the diocesan synods fell into abeyance, this was because there had come to be a body of ecclesiastical Custom framed in the Councils of the Church: the bishop was still a constitutional and not a personal ruler. We do not, of course, contend that there have never been capricious or tyrannical bishops, but only that the system of government is constitutional in its character: the bishop is an executive officer, who is to carry out, as wisely as he can, the rules which Christian experience has framed.

He also has another duty; it has been through the mutual counsel and advice of the bishops of provinces, or of nations, or even of the whole world, that the experience of the Church has been gathered and consolidated. The authority of such general Councils lies not in the decree, but in the weight of evidence gathered from all parts of the world: the bishops, in constant communication with the people of their dioceses, have been the most suitable instruments for expressing the sense of Christian men throughout the world; and thus the canon of the Bible and the creeds attained to a final settlement. The recent expressions of the Custom of the Church at the meetings of all Anglican bishops have not been unimportant, because no formal enactment has been passed.

But of all episcopal duties, the most important are those, by exercising which, he provides for the continuance of teaching and ministering in the Church. It is his duty to examine into the conversation and attainments of candidates applying for Holy Orders; and if he is satisfied, to commit to them the sacred trust which Jesus bestowed upon the apostles. It is thus that the continued life of the Church can be preserved. In this he is assisted by the presbyters around him, and by the witness of the people assembled together and solemnly adjured.

We have thus seen that there is a practically universal consent as to the existence of the various clerical duties which have been discriminated: as a matter of fact, the duties of ruling have been generally committed to bishops. If it be true that Church administration can be better carried on by committees and delegates than by one responsible individual, this is only true of Church administration, and not of any other affairs whatever. We may fairly contend that the system which has grown up under the experience of eighteen centuries seems to be as likely to conduce to good government as any other that has been devised. Personal administration is likely to afford the most effective discipline, and what is equally important, the most effective means for encouraging the clergy in their difficulties. It is the place of the bishop to lighten the labours of his clergy, to work with them for the good of the Church, not merely to correct the errors that may occur; and no committee or court can exercise such care as this so effectively, if at all. That system which calls forth the greatest amount of the sense of personal responsibility is likely to be the most effective.

Arguing thus on the mere grounds of expediency, we may contend that the episcopal system is the one which is most likely to be successful in the present day. There are infinitely stronger arguments in its support when we think of the episcopate as the means of maintaining Christian teaching and ministering from generation to generation. No other system has had such a trial as this; none can pretend to such success. Wesleyanism is swayed with every wind of popular preaching. Presbyterianism has found much difficulty in maintaining conformity even to its own Calvinistic creed. It is currently stated that 'orthodoxy' is fast falling to pieces in Scotland. Be this as it may, we may well contend that no other system has so succeeded in treasuring and maintaining the Catholic faith.

If there be no probable gain in departing from the ancient government of the Church, there is much certain loss. Believing as we do in the unity of the Church, as an ideal, we hold firmly to that episcopate by which the unity has been approximately actualised. It is through the episcopate that the experience of the Church is consolidated. It is the episcopate that, as a living power, has linked the Church of to-day with the Church of the first century. In so far as unity has been approximately attained, it has been through this divine order. Thus it is, that while we cherish a faith in one Catholic and Apostolic Church, the experience of all ages gives us help in determining that there is most hope for its realisation in loyalty to the episcopal system.

At the same time, we cannot forget that the political powers and social status of the bishops of Western Christendom have seemed to many men to be incompatible with the effective discharge of their Christian duties: we have only insisted on the episcopate as an instrument of fulfilling certain Christian duties; we must sketch very briefly the changes of form which that office has undergone, in order to see clearly what kind of episcopate is best suited for the discharge of the duty of ruling the Church in India.

II. *Various Forms of the Episcopate.*

The broad outlines of the episcopal system have been already described. Religious experience testifies to its value in some form, and testifies also to its peculiar adaptability to very different states of society.

1. The ideal of Greek political life centred in the city; all their institutions were really municipal; in many cases the old freedom had entirely expired before the spreading of Christianity, but this was not so in the province of Asia. Ephesus and the other cities there had preserved a certain amount of autonomy, and the delegates went to and fro to express the desires of the city to the sovereign senate at Rome. It was not strange that the constitution of the Church should come to be municipal also, and that each bishop should be regarded as ruling in his own city.

2. In Syria, on the other hand, there was no similar political tradition; the bishop

ruled, we may say, like a satrap over the Christians scattered through the wide area.[1] In Egypt also this was the case, though as time passed on the Asian system of appointing a bishop in each important town came to be adopted.

3. There appears to have been a peculiarity in the civic episcopate of Asia, for the duties of the bishop were so closely confined to his own town that the Christians in the neighbouring villages were not properly superintended: we thus find in Asia the institution of village bishops. It is of course possible, as Dr. Lightfoot suggests, that this institution was a survival of a primitive condition when the duties of presbyter and bishop were not definitely severed.[2] None the less is it true that when the separation became marked, the 'bishop' was such a purely civic functionary that the oversight of the village Christians was retained in presbyterial hands. The system was deeply rooted, for it seems to have reappeared in the daughter Churches of Asia, at Lyons

[1] Sozomen, vii. 19.

[2] *Philippians*: 'On the Christian Ministry.'

and Vienne, and to have continued in Gaul for many centuries. The spirit of the age of Charlemagne and his successors was against the village bishops,[1] but they had been recognised as a useful institution at an earlier date, and might have continued for long had any one succeeded in defining their relation to the bishop of the neighbouring city.

4. In the other provinces of the Roman empire, where each city was the administrative centre of a district carefully defined, we find a still different form of the episcopate: it is territorial, the bishop's sway extending over a province. We may consider this as the model which Cyprian had in his mind. In Asia there must have been many interlacing jurisdictions, but Cyprian has a clear idea of a diocese in which was one bishop, and refusal to communicate with the bishop was the one clear mark of schism. Distinct jurisdictions within the same area were, from his point of view, incompatible with Church unity; and his conception of episcopacy, as

[1] Weizsäcker, *Kampf gegen den Chorepiscopat des frankischen Reichs*, p. 8.

always coupled with territorial jurisdiction, harmonising as it did with the imperial system of Rome, came to be characteristic of Latin Christianity.

5. Another form of episcopacy obtained in the Scottish Church. This Church was wholly monastic in its character.[1] The great monastery at Hy had dependants all over the country, and the abbot of the mother was supreme over the whole of the daughter institutions; but this abbot might be a presbyter or deacon, or very frequently a layman; sometimes in the days of decadence he was not even a monk. In every case his position was due to his hereditary connexion with the man who had founded the monastery and granted its lands at first. The principal duties of ruling lay with the abbot, but in each monastery there were one or more, perhaps many bishops. Their learning was their chief qualification, but they alone ordained, and they were the chief ministers. Their purely episcopal functions were preserved, even if they seem to us to be strangely

[1] Skene, *Celtic Scotland*, ii. 42. Compare also Reeves, *Adamnan*, 654; and Todd, *Life of St. Patrick*, Introd.

circumscribed by the fact that they had no dioceses and no definite jurisdiction.

6. Merely titular bishops may be passed over: this class has existed at different times,[1] but their existence has always given rise to confusion.

7. One other class only need be mentioned, the tribal bishop, who had a definite jurisdiction, which, however, extended not over an area, but over a tribe, in whatever place they may be found. Such appears to have been the position of Ulphilas[2] among the Goths.

These seven different classes may be grouped by the broad distinction between bishops who had, and bishops who had not, a definite jurisdiction. The first class may be left out of account as not different—for our purpose—from the fourth; these have been mentioned separately, because there seems to be some ground for believing that the growth of episcopacy was different in the two cases. The monastic and titular

[1] Sozomen, vi. 34; Mabillon, *Acta Sanctorum Ordinis S. Benedicti*, iii. pref. p. xiii.

[2] Sozomen, vi. 37.

bishops may be put together as having no jurisdiction. On the other hand, the municipal, village, and tribal bishops had all definite jurisdictions: they might have acted in concert, and probably did so act in the East, with their relationships defined; but the claims of the territorial bishops were incompatible with the admission of any other authority; and terrible trouble arose in Gaul over the question of cross jurisdiction, and of the intrusion of monastic (or even of merely titular) bishops into provinces that were already effectively administered. How far these different forms of the episcopate are really compatible in the same district may be discussed below; at present it may suffice to say that, so far as one can judge, only the territorial system gave such solidarity to the episcopate as to make it able to preserve the Church from the disorders of those days; but, necessary as the suppression of any other form of the office may have been at that time, we cannot feel that such suppression was necessary for all time.

This brief review may serve to substantiate the opinion expressed above, that the episcopate may be rendered congruent to almost any stage of social and political development. It takes different forms among Greek and Roman and Gothic peoples; it may be different as a missionary and as an administrative institution. It is evident that the civic episcopacy of Asia would have been impossible among the Gothic tribes, or in the monastic Scottish Church; and we may lay it down as a settled principle, that *the best form of the episcopate, at any place and time, is that which is most congruent to the particular society in which the Church is planted.*

A few illustrations of this may suffice. One of the most striking facts in the history of Christianity is the rapid conversion of the English people so soon after their settlement in this country. We are all acquainted with the complete plan which Gregory sketched, based on the old imperial divisions, for two ecclesiastical provinces, with their different constituent dioceses. That has never been carried out, and it was soon found necessary to waive it, and attach Christianity to the tribal kingdoms rather than to territorial divisions. The bishops and clergy took their place among the thegns—the personal dependants of the king,[1] and thus found a place in the life of each of the English tribes. It was in later days that the landed settlement of England was completed, and that thegns and freemen were alike attached to the land, so that the ecclesiastical, like the royal jurisdiction, came to be defined by territorial bounds. But when the English sent forth missionaries to their cousins on the Continent, we find a return to the simpler ecclesiastical structure. S. Boniface was a bishop of the nation; he was the ruler of the men, not of their land. In Germany, too, the tribal episcopate flourished, till at length, with the settlement of the tribes, it also became territorial.

With these successes we may contrast the miserable failure of another mission. Any reader of S. Bernard's life must recall the story of the interesting friendship which he formed with the Irish monk, S. Malachy, and the terrible impression of the misgovernment of the Irish Church which his

[1] Kemble, *Saxons in England*, II. chaps. viii. ix.

friend's story made on his mind. As the recognised leader of Christian thought at his time, he denounced the degradation into which the monastic Church in Ireland had fallen; and thus it was that he gave the religious excuse which was needed to sanction the schemes of conquest that Henry II. was forming. The expeditions of that monarch resulted in the establishment of a feudal nobility and of a feudal episcopacy, and seven centuries of misery tell us how far either institution has succeeded in gaining a hold on the Celtic people. That that people was not a bad subject for missionary labour was sufficiently shown by the success of the earlier saints and of the emissaries of Rome at a later time; but the territorial episcopacy had no point of contact with the life of the Celtic tribes, and the Irish Church of Henry II. has ever been regarded as a foreign institution that had no real place in the hearts of the nation.

A somewhat similar remark might be made about Scotland. The objection of the men of the seventeenth century was not to an episcopate, but to an episcopate that was under royal rather than popular influence. The Scotch people had never enjoyed any real political life. In the halcyon-days of Alexander III., the mercantile classes had preferred to hold their own as a separate class in the convention of burghs and Scotch Hanse, rather than claim a share in the Parliamentary representation; and as a consequence, the people had no real voice in that assembly. When, at the Reformation, the Genevan system was introduced into the country, the ecclesiastical assemblies became the place for the assertion of popular liberties: in them the king was but a 'silly' vassal. Thus it was that Presbyterianism could put itself forward as the organ of self-government; it was only, however, when Laud hurried on[1] the needed reforms by royal mandate, instead of by means of the synods of the Church, that episcopacy came to be obviously identical with a personal government, as presbytery had appeared to be with self-government. How utterly mistaken the latter opinion was, was keenly felt by Milton and his contemporaries, who

[1] Heylin's *Life of Laud*, p. 322.

denounced an oligarchy which was fundamentally opposed to any true liberty. But the colour which was given to episcopacy by the unconstitutional action of Laud, against which the Scottish bishops wisely protested, rendered any form of it incongruous with the new political life of the people.

Our survey of religious experience has led us to maintain these three principles :—

1. That episcopacy in some form or other is the kind of administration most likely to be successful, and the only one which holds out a hope for the ultimate realisation of Church unity.

2. That episcopacy has existed in many different forms in different places ; and,

3. That, if we wish success to attend our efforts in any land, we must be careful to establish that form of episcopacy which is most congruent to the life of the people.

III. *Membership of the Church.*

So far we have considered the government of the Church ; but the due organisation of the body always implies the exercise of care in regard to the admission of new members. It is in this point that the difference between the two views of Christianity, to which we alluded in the last chapter, comes into prominence. Those who think of the Church as composed of real believers, will insist that each individual who is received should make a full statement of his own personal faith and religious experience, so that it may be possible to judge whether he is worthy of a place in the Christian community. Those, on the other hand, who regard the Church as a great body which holds an ideal before her members and provides them means for realising it, will require in the new members, not a proof of actual attainment, but the expression of a desire that they should have a part in this great society, and a guarantee that they know the meaning of the Christian profession. It is not only the saints of God who form the Church; from the point of view we have adopted, none can be refused admission if there is a sincere desire for a part in the life of the Church, and a guarantee that this desire is an intelligent one. Nor need there be, where the society is firmly planted, any difficulty in receiving those children whom sponsors solemnly desire to be brought up as members of Christ, while they pledge themselves to instruct them in their responsibilities and privileges as citizens of the kingdom of God upon earth; the weight of Christian experience in favour of infant baptism is excessively strong. But the question of the admission of members becomes one of much greater difficulty in missionary churches where we have to consider the training of those who have had no early Christian impressions that were deepened by after years, but who must be tested both as to the reality of their desire to embrace the Christian life and as to their understanding of all that it involves.

We cannot doubt that in many cases the Church has not been sufficiently careful in this respect. Passing over the scandals of the Spanish conquest in America, we must feel that there was a great carelessness about the instruction of converts, when tribes embraced the new religion on the mere example of their kings; it is in earlier days, while paganism was still dominant, that we notice the greatest care in the instruction of those who desired admission to the Church. As abuses crept in, there were more and more stringent regulations made for catechumens; and in Alexandria, at the time of Origen, they passed through three different stages; in the earliest they did not attend the common assemblies or public instructions of the Church at all, but were attached to Christian households where they might get the best initiation into the daily life of the Christian man.[1] The other regulations and distinctions do not so nearly concern us, as they appear to have been specially designed with the view of preventing spies and informers from attending the worship of the Church, with the purpose of then denouncing the Christians to Pagan persecutors. Family religion was treated not as by any means a substitute for, but as a propaedeutic to, the worship of the Church, both for infants and for adults who sought to be received into the Church; and when in the disorder of the dark ages family life had lost most of its security, the Bene-

[1] Rothe, *De disciplinâ arcani*, §§ 4, 5.

dictine cloisters formed an excellent school for training men for a Christian profession in the great world. While we would never undervalue the influence of Christian teaching, we would yet contend that the religious experience of all ages shows that it is by the insensible action of a Christian atmosphere that the Christian character, whether of an infant or of a convert, may be best formed. Church organisation can never be complete if, with the most ample provision for preaching and instruction, there is no care for habituating the members of the Church in active Christian life.

VI.

APPLICATION OF THESE PRINCIPLES TO INDIA.

I. *The Problem stated.*

HAVING attained a general knowledge of the principles on which Church organisation should proceed, we must now endeavour to apply them to the special circumstances of India. An attempt to delineate the difficulties that lie before us will be the first step to accomplishing their removal; a full account of these difficulties would be a history of the various races of India, and of the long succession of conquests which have taken place on that peninsula, while it would also involve a complete account of the different bodies of professing Christians who have sent missionaries there. We do not propose to undertake any such task as this, but shall only endeavour to bring the most important points into clear relief.

It will be a help, too, to limit the inquiry at once by indicating the matters which seem to need no further discussion at present; such is the question as to the relation of various bodies of professing Christians to one another. This may be omitted here,—not because it is an unimportant matter in India, but because it is not special to India. All over the world the same difficulty occurs, and we can look for no special solution in any one quarter. In the preceding pages of this essay an effort has been made to show where the solution lies. The Catholic Experience of baptized men furnishes objective facts to which an appeal can be made; nor is any other common ground conceivable; to appeal to aught else than this is to appeal to an arbitrarily limited body of religious experience, and to bow before this as a constituted authority, rather than to take universal Christian experience as giving the evidence on which to form our own judgments. In so far as different bodies of Christians are striving to realise God's kingdom on earth, it is obvious that they must work in a common direction; in so far as men are working with a reverent regard to Christian experience in all ages, they are likely to be working wisely and successfully. We must first ask what plan is most likely to suit the needs of India; we shall then be in a position to judge to what extent the methods adopted by various bodies of Christians can be expected to combine with the system that most completely commends itself.

The chief difficulty lies in the fact that Christianity comes before the native mind as the badge of a victorious and hated race: of the hatred we fear there can be no doubt. The Mutiny was an evidence of it that will not soon be forgotten; and even if we leave out of account the rumours of disaffection which were current at the time when the imperial dignity was assumed by the Queen, and which have become louder since the recent troubles on the borders of the territory, we should find in the measures which have been taken with regard to the native press a sufficient proof that our Government does not regard itself as a popular institution. On the vexed question whether this unpopularity is deserved or not we shall not enter; for our immediate purpose this is a matter of little moment: so long as the English rule is unpopular, so too will be the religion which Englishmen teach. Occasional displays of benevolence in time of famine may have proved the existence of kind feeling towards the natives, without removing the unfortunate impression which is caused by English rule, and which cannot be easily dispelled. For while no one will contend that our great dependency is ruled with such total disregard of its interests as marked the home Government in its relations with our American colonies during the eighteenth century, there are still cases when the good of the Eastern Empire is sacrificed to the interests of Lancashire manufacturers.[1] Under the plea of opening up the country, large sums are expended on works that benefit the English in India rather than the native population, while the transition from Eastern

[1] Sime, *Outlines of an Industrial Science*, p. 74.

to Western ways[1] is accompanied with much evil that may, we hope, ultimately pass away. All the hatred of conquerors, all the antipathy against innovations, all the jealousy of a capitalist class, must be outlived before the English rule can be popular in India, or the Christian religion be welcomed, as it was in some of the South Sea Islands, because it is English. Anglo-Indians in military stations and planters' districts are provided with chaplains; and while we cannot wish that the English in India should be dissociated from the Christian profession, they too often bring discredit upon it by unchristian lives and overbearing conduct.

Other great difficulties arise from the disintegration of the native population. We have hinted at defects in the English Government, but we doubt if any reasonable critic sees, for the present, any hope of a better; certainly the native population is not capable of self-government, because it is so terribly disorganised. Western culture has done

[1] The decay of village tribunals and introduction of the English judicial system afford opportunities for perjury unknown before.

much in the way of breaking down old religious and moral ties, and has done little to supply new ones. Caste and the suttee are abominable institutions, but it seems a doubtful benefit to replace them by socialistic principles, or by a purely non-religious view of marriage as a mere civil contract. 'Young Bengal' shows little sign of coming to form a useful wealthy class in the community. When we glance at the poorer inhabitants, we see no signs of any training in self-government in either town or country, if we except those districts where the village system has been preserved as the basis of land tenure; and with our experience of the decay of that system everywhere in Europe[1] —even in Russia,—we can hardly expect that it will hold its own as a permanent element in Indian civilisation. Looking at the native population, we find no social organism, only a chaotic ferment. This is another very great difficulty in the way of the spread of Christianity. In other days it has been most successful where it has grafted itself on existent social institutions; at first on the syna-

[1] Lavelaye, *Primitive Property, passim.*

gogue system of the Jews of Judea and the Dispersion; in our own island on the power of the tribal kings; but in India there is no social system on which the religious institutions of Christianity can be grafted. In such a wide country, thus socially disintegrated, that form of Christianity may be expected to succeed best which is most readily adaptable, so that it may easily affiliate itself to the different elements that exist side by side but uncombined.

These various elements may be best distinguished by considering the various races that have found a home on Indian soil. We need not pretend to enumerate these, but only to indicate the chief divisions, to classify them as the aborigines, such as the Santals and hill tribes, the Sanscrit-speaking race, the Mussulman, and the scattered Parsee, Jew, and other foreign races. To all of these the Church has a message;—there is a place for them all in the kingdom of God; but while she has a message for all, she must appeal to each, and be ready to adapt herself to the special requirements of each people. If there are no similar positive elements all over India to which Christianity can ally itself, there may be positive elements in many separate quarters; but one plain principle remains for our guidance, to present Christianity, so far as possible, in a form which is compatible with native social instincts. This is not to commend a dangerous 'economy,' but only to insist on a judicious adaptation of the pure faith and the tried constitution of the Church to new social surroundings.

One other difficulty must be faced. It is sufficiently difficult for a Church to maintain by voluntary contributions all the agencies that are needed for the carrying on of her work, but this is wholly impossible in a missionary Church when the number of presbyters and other officers bears a specially large proportion to the number of members. A native Church among the impoverished millions of India must be at least partially dependent on extraneous help, and this help will be doubtless supplied in the future, as it has been in the past, by European missionary societies. It is not unnatural that those who contribute a large proportion of the funds should demand a considerable voice in regard to the employment of the money they raise, and a most important question arises as to the relation of these home committees to an organised native Church. This is indeed a different matter from the difficulties we have indicated above: it has to do with the pecuniary support of the Church, not directly with its religious life and organisation. For all that, the difficulty is a real one, and cannot be ignored.

II. *A suggested solution.*

We are now in a position to discuss in what way the principles which have been gathered from the Christian experience of the past can be most suitably applied to the native population of India. It is at once obvious that the episcopate, as it has till recently existed, does not at all satisfy the requirements of the case. Attached to great territorial divisions, and directly associated with English rule, there is no common ground of sympathy between the heathen native tribes and bishops who share the unpopularity of all that is English.

A further difficulty lies in the fact that the Indian dioceses, for their due working, involve the possession of unusual linguistic powers. It is not every man who can acquire the power of preaching four sermons in four different languages on one day. Besides this, the territorial dioceses are not in other respects homogeneous, and it would be very difficult to apply the same principles to all the districts they include. The circumstances of the English and native congregations are so different, that it would be impossible to find any approach to a consensus among them in regard to many details of worship and discipline. A diocesan synod where native and English clergy sat side by side would not be likely to devise what was best for the native congregations. If an elaborate worship is a cause of offence to them, it may be better to dispense with it, while it would be injurious to the English to deprive them of devotional aids to which they have been accustomed. So, too, with matters of discipline; personal care and intimate knowledge of circumstances are needed to tell what conformity to our customs in regard to social matters is desirable, and to draw a line between what is permissible and what is wrong. In all these matters the experience of well instructed native Christians, or of those missionaries who are constantly dealing with natives, is what we need. For the best administration of the Church we need to have 'tribal'[1] bishops, whose jurisdiction shall extend over a certain *sept or race*, in whatever place they are found; not territorial bishops, whose jurisdiction extends over a certain *area* whatever races it may contain.

It may appear at first sight that this would be the mere cultivation of schism—the intrusion of a new bishop to exercise episcopal functions within a diocese already formed—and doubtless this would be the case if their respective jurisdictions were left indefinite; but there need be no intrusion, no interference of one with another, if their respective jurisdictions are clearly defined and evidently understood. Trouble arises when the relation-

[1] Linguistic bishops might be a better term in a country where tribal ties are so slightly felt.

ship of any two authorities is ill-defined or misunderstood, as, *e.g.*, if there is doubt about the boundary between two countries, and how far the rights of each of two sovereigns extend. But where there is no confusion there need be no interference in each other's spheres. The 'tribal' bishop rules over the Christians and provides for the heathen of a certain race and language, say, for simplicity sake, within the diocese of Bombay: there might be half a dozen such 'tribal' bishops, all exercising their functions within the same area, side by side, and not interfering with one another, and the bishop of Bombay could still retain his authority over all races not otherwise provided for. We should have a number of co-ordinate episcopates, not as divisions among Christians, but as branches of one Church. The ground of difference would not be religious opinion, but difference of race and language. This is the real means of avoiding schism: to recognise the natural differences among men as the basis on which the one ecclesiastical organisation is reared. Schism implies the separation of one Christian from another on account of religious opinion ; but co-ordinate Churches, which only differ because of the differences of race and language, would be, and would feel themselves to be, fundamentally one. Each bishop would be assisted by his synod in the affairs of his own Church, and would rule that branch of the Church as its special needs required. But all these bishops would meet in provincial synods for the hearing of appeals: so long as the various branches were in full communion with each other, so long as all gathered together in the same synods, the co-ordinate episcopates would be obviously parts of one body.

It may be said that this would lead to an unnecessary multiplication of agencies. In many quarters the district chaplain (English) might assist in appealing to the native population around: the same edifice may serve for two different bodies of worshippers. Nor do we see why this should not still be the case; the same presbyter might hold the licence of the bishop of Bombay to minister to the English population, and also the licence of the 'tribal' bishop to care for the natives in the place. Such a presbyter would owe obedience to both bishops, and have a place in both synods.

If we are right in believing that this system has been in actual use in the East,[1] we need not stop to inquire whether any canonical objection can be urged against it; but we apprehend that the canons, which appear to condemn it, were framed to meet intrusion in another's jurisdiction, and that no valid argument can be brought against establishing co-ordinate episcopates within the same area, so long as their jurisdiction can be defined. It might perhaps be only a temporary matter. As education extends, the native languages may die out, as Cornish, Irish, Manx, and Gaelic die out before English. As race differences thus disappeared, the dioceses might be re-arranged, and territorial divisions might be the final form in India as elsewhere; but yet so long as these marked differences of race and language continue, the 'tribal' episcopates would have a useful part to play.

[1] This may be deduced from a consideration of the Canons of the Councils of Laodicea, Antioch, Ancyra, Sardica. Cf. Spelman.

How useful, it is hardly possible to estimate: each of these disorganised tribes might find a new centre, round which the elements of their national life would rally: they might find in their bishop a true father of the people, who cared for their highest interests, and who identified himself with them. They would find themselves called to rally round him and strengthen him by their counsels; they would feel the responsibility of taking their part in the ordination of priests or the election of bishops: new interests would be awakened, and all their tribal instincts, all their sympathy for men of the same race and language, would be enlisted on behalf of an institution which was their own. For if godliness has promise of the life that is to come, it has assuredly the best promise for the life that now is. These down-trodden, depressed peoples may be awakened to a sense of the value of human life here, and to the power of regulating it wisely. Association for the good of their fellows, a sense of responsibility for the spreading of Christ's kingdom, practice in the administration of affairs, these are the benefits which would follow from committing to nations the management of their own Church; from sending to them their own bishops, from calling on their own presbyters to assist him by their counsel, and summoning, if it be possible, representatives of the laity also to elect to places of trust and to help in questions of finance. Thus might a true Christian civilisation be developed; underneath the military imperialism and secular tribunals of England, an organised religious polity would grow up, one in its aims and its life, but yet deeply rooted in the hearts of the natives. We know what a hold their own religious forms have upon the Welsh and the Irish; we know how these two races have refused to adopt the religious system of their conqueror. Well will it be for Christianity if this disaster can be avoided abroad,—if we can give the subject races a true religion that they shall feel is their own, and be able to identify with themselves, while it yet forms a tie between East and West, so that as of old the masters and the conquered shall be one in Christ Jesus; the various parts of that organism would be independent and self-regulating by their synods, while yet the episcopate formed a living link which bound them together in one body, not merely fostered in each branch the same spirit.

We believe, too, that the mere existence of such 'tribal' bishops, ruling with the assistance of their synods, would remove some of the difficulties which have arisen between home committees and authorities abroad. The committees have believed that they were advancing the interests of the native Christians, where these might be disregarded by men whose chief work lay with the English residents and not in a mission field proper. But a native (or missionary) bishop who acted with the council of his native (or missionary) presbyters, need not fear that his hands will not be strengthened by help from home. As time goes on we may hope that the voluntary gifts of the natives to their own Church would be more and more sufficient, and that the various financial difficulties would be faced and discussed in a diocesan council of clergy and laity. The more the bishop can lead his people to take an active part in Church work, the more independent will he become of any possible misunderstanding on the part of friends in England.

Such is an attempt to sketch a possible solution of the various difficulties which were described above: the formation of small 'tribal' episcopates, which would yet be but different members of one body, and whose mutual relations might be clear enough, while each might become a new centre of civilisation and social life, which each depressed population might feel to be their own,—this would remove the barrier which is raised by English unpopularity. But a not less important matter is the development of synodic action and of councils: this must remove the possibility of arbitrary rule—a greater evil than even unwise rule would be; while it would call forth the interests and energies of the clergy and laity in the cause of Christ, and the cause of their own folk. The value of such action has been most fully demonstrated in the great revival of vigour in the Scottish Church of the Anglican communion. The

Code of Canons which has been formulated, and the practice of the Representative Council, might well be models for any Church, tribal or territorial, at home or abroad.

If this be an ideal of Church life for India, in what way might various Christian bodies co-operate in bringing it about? We cannot tell how far they would so co-operate, but we do believe that branches of the Catholic Church thus organised would outlive any other body; the fittest would survive. Our question is, How far might they co-operate in this direction? So far as the Anglican communion is concerned, there would be a need for a division of dioceses, not by territorial limits, but by withdrawing the native populations—or definite portions of them—from the jurisdiction of the territorial bishops, and instituting 'tribal' bishoprics by their side. The development of diocesan synods would be the first duty of each of the 'tribal' bishops. It might be urged, perhaps, that the appointment of missionary suffragans, like Bishops Caldwell and Sargant, would suffice: and that this is a great step in advance, none can doubt who has read of the warmth of their reception among their people, of the vigour of the Church life in their districts, and of the Councils they have gathered around them. All this is indeed a great movement in the right direction, and perhaps the time is hardly ripe for going the length we should like to see, and recognising the chief pastors of the native Church, not merely as assistant bishops in certain districts of a large diocese, but as independent members of the episcopal College in these lands. Their position as mere suffragans in special districts does not solve the difficulty, for the native Christians in the chief towns of the diocese have no part in the native Church organisation; the territorial bishop administers the ecclesiastical affairs of the mass of the English and of some scattered native congregations; the suffragan superintends the native population, which is thickly gathered in his own district; but those native Christians who are most exposed to the chilling contempt and pride of race of Anglo-Indians have special need of the countenance and sympathy of a bishop of their own. The position which is given to the chief pastors of the native Christians as mere assistant bishops in a limited district of a territorial diocese, does not allow of that self-dependent action of the 'tribal' Church which we believe to be essential to its growth. Can we hope that our bishops would promote, or that Government would permit, a self-denying ordinance which would render the 'tribal' Church entirely independent of territorial jurisdiction?

There are other matters in which all professing Christians can co-operate in securing free play for the growth of a native civilisation. A wise policy was sketched out in 1854 when the Government set itself to foster and direct local educational efforts rather than attempt to start and maintain colleges itself.[1] This policy, if persistently carried out, would encourage the self-development of the native populations in various directions; it would foster growth, and would stimulate the founding of non-religious, or Parsee, or Brahmin, or Christian

[1] Johnston, *Our Educational Policy in India*, p. 18.

Colleges where there was need felt and energy to meet that need. But recently the Government in Bengal has departed from this line; it has itself undertaken the founding of such colleges, and has thus repressed local effort, while by founding non-religious colleges it authoritatively encourages a non-religious education, to the practical exclusion of any other line of teaching. Such State interference is as much opposed to the doctrines of the popular political philosophy expounded by Mr. Herbert Spencer, as it is to the wishes of those who have the extension of the Church at heart. Financially extravagant, dwarfing local efforts—a recent attempt at Delhi being the sole exception—and giving an authoritative encouragement to non-religious education, the action of the Government surely demands the opposition of all men who have at heart the self-development of our Indian population, let alone its Christianisation. Even those who, by their repudiation of the ideal of a visible kingdom of God, have cut themselves off from an interest in extending the Church, may surely co-operate in opposing the mistaken direction in which the action of Government is tending.

If Independents may go with us in this, and in such movements as this, still more help may be expected from Presbyterians. Their presbyteries need not sensibly differ from diocesan conferences and synods, and those who had been trained in the one would soon find their place in the other. In what way the path may be prepared for the re-absorption of Presbyterians into the Church need not be here considered, for it is a question which must be settled in Scotland before the solution can be applied in India.

It is from Wesleyanism that we can hope for the most complete co-operation with the work of the Church. The class system offers an invaluable form for practical Christian training. Applied by them to the edification of members, it would fill a most useful place in the training of catechumens. If it be difficult to find Christian homes in which candidates for baptism may be received, it may certainly be possible to find leaders by whom their habits may be formed and their aspirations guided. So, too, the organisation of Methodism is by no means inharmonious with the organisation of the Catholic Church as recommended by Catholic experience.

For to Catholic experience we must ever hold fast, looking for light to make it our own, and for wisdom to work on its lines. In the growth and consolidation of that experience is our hope for the realisation of our ideal—the spread of the one kingdom of God. Some who have despaired of its attainment may yet aid us in bringing it in; others who have chosen their own methods of working are yet, unconsciously perhaps, co-operating with us—co-operating with us in the effort not merely to save individual souls, but to regenerate the life of the native populations.

For accomplishing this in India, as for maintaining a nobler life at home, Christianity is the essential condition. It is easy to sneer that 'a native converted is a native spoiled,' and to point out that missionaries have come for the fall of many in India; but not less truly have they come for a great arising. Civil and military officials, whose sole interests lie in the smooth administration of an alien rule, cannot fairly judge of endeavours, with which they have little sympathy, to rear a Christian civilisation among the subject races, and thus to fit them for taking their place as one of the nations of the world. In days gone by the Church raised one mighty empire which controlled the contending passions of feudal barons, and preserved all that was noblest in Europe by guarding it; and it is to the Church that we look as the only body that, devoid of commercial interests and military ambition, has the will as well as the power to foster the growth of free political life among the populations of India.

NOTES.

S. PAUL AND MORAL INDIFFERENTISM.

PAGE 6.

Let every man be fully persuaded in his own mind. The statement which is sometimes made that these words merely apply to 'non-essentials,' seems to me to involve a complete misapprehension of the force of the apostle's argument, as well as a misunderstanding of the circumstances of the times. It is an important question in regard to the whole teaching of the apostle. On the one hand, he is represented as looking down from the heights of his spiritual attainments on the petty squabbles of the converts, and telling them that some matters were so very trivial that they might use their own judgment, as they could not go far wrong. On the other hand, it may be contended that S. Paul was deciding these cases of conscience by means of a principle of much wider application, and one that was effecting a revolution in the current morality of his friends.

It is no easy matter for us, looking back from a distance of eighteen hundred years, to realise the extent of the revolution which took place in the minds of religious men during the first century. The God-fearing man of that day had been brought up in the strict acceptance of a certain *code* of duty,—duties as to his personal habits—what he ate, and drank, and put on; duties as to his neighbours—honesty and uprightness; duties to God—reverence, and obedience, and frequent worship; all these various duties had been authoritatively enjoined, all had been hallowed by the reverent tradition of ages, and the deeds were all alike done by the pious believer, not because they in any way commended themselves to his personal convictions, but because they had been authoritatively commanded by God when He gave His people a complete code of right action.

It was, however, practically impossible for the Jews of the Dispersion, and still more so for those Gentiles who accepted the salvation that was revealed by the Messiah, to live in accordance with the definite regulations of that Divine code. Some lost heart at the effort and fell from the faith; some were skilled in petty evasions and non-natural interpretations which served as excuses; all were in danger of sinking into moral indifferentism and open licence. It was then that the world was ripe for the preaching of that new principle which is so plainly put forth by S. Paul, that men are to be made righteous, not by vainly seeking to regulate their conduct according to an impracticable code, but by following the dictates of an inner principle, so that their thought and speech and action may all be formed by the indwelling Christ;—in theological language, they are to be justified by faith, not by the works of the law.

To say that the struggle of these times was as to the continued bindingness of the *ceremonial* law is to take a most superficial view of the matter; it is to look only at the field where the battle was fought, and to ignore the forces that were engaged and the issue that was involved. For this was not merely a controversy as to this or that particular duty,—circumcision or Sabbath observance; it was a struggle as to the whole nature of morality and the sanctions under which every duty was to be done. Men were in doubt as to whether the highest rule of right was to be found in the regulations of a definite code, or in the guidance of a good Spirit. They wondered about the obligation of Morality, and as to whether actions were to be done, however unmeaning or irksome they might seem, because they had been authoritatively commanded of old; or whether, on the other hand, each individual, regenerated in baptism and enlightened by God's Holy Spirit, might seek to make his whole being the express image of the life that is hid with Christ in God? They asked themselves, too, what was the truest motive for God-fearing; was each man bound to serve the Lord, not out of mere fear for the thunders of Sinai, but because the love of Christ was constraining him? Nor, bitter though the struggle was, did the issue remain long doubtful. Religious men came everywhere at length to recognise that morality is not to be shaped by any authoritative impracticable code, but is the free outcome of the Christian Consciousness.

Such was the revolution: let us now look more closely at S. Paul's argument. In the first place, we may notice that he calls attention to the inner motive of duty—regarding the day unto the Lord. This was passing beyond the point of view of the opposite party. The law enjoined external conduct, and its most scrupulous observers were satisfied by mere external conduct. S. Paul decides the case of conscience by showing that there is another standard than the Mosaic Law to which the question may be referred. He is going beyond the position of the Judaisers.

Yet he is doing no despite to the law. Sabbath observance was distinctly commanded in the Mosaic code. With all his boldness we can hardly imagine the apostle setting up his *ipse dixit* in opposition to the thunders of Sinai, and asserting that anything which was there commanded was of no importance. Had he attempted to do so, it would have been necessary to draw a line and say which of the laws were still binding, and which were about unimportant matters, in regard to which men might do as they liked. But he makes no such attempt: there is no mention of any criterion by which to distinguish essentials from non-essentials; he simply advises that each man should seek to render his conduct pure by living in the consciousness of the unseen Christ; by such faith he might become a partaker in the righteousness of Christ, and all his deeds, trivial or not, be done unto the Lord. It was through the common decision of men who were seeking thus to live, that a new scheme of duties came to be regarded as binding on the people of God,—a scheme which neglected many outward observances, but which set forth an ideal that was very difficult of attainment.

Starting from this high conception of the whole of life as devoted to God, it was impossible for S. Paul to regard any piece of conduct as too trivial to be either right or wrong. According to him every little deed was right or wrong, was of faith or sin, according as it was or was not done unto the Lord; and the words before us find their echo in numberless passages in his epistles. Those who maintain that aught in human life is so colourless as to be neither right nor wrong, must seek for support elsewhere than in the teaching of the apostle of the Gentiles.

Nor as we look back can we doubt that in thus appealing from the Sinaitic code to the conscience of the Christian man, S. Paul was placing morality on a firmer foundation. What served as a criterion in cases of conscience was assuredly a sound basis for all morality, as the scheme of life that grew up from the common convictions of conscientious Christian men was the noblest the world had seen. Judged either by the area over which it was influential, or by its effectiveness in the lives of individuals and peoples, we may say that the code of Sinai, with all its terrible sanctions, was but a feeble guardian of morality when contrasted with the living and deepening Christian Consciousness.

CATHOLIC EXPERIENCE AND COMMON SENSE.

PAGE 20.

IN making appeal to man's religious experience we are not claiming the 'common consent of mankind' in favour of any opinion. Whether there be tribes that are wholly devoid of any sense of worship or not, there can be no doubt that even if the suffrage of the race were to declare that there is a God, this would be a mere abstract proposition, and that any attempt to describe His nature or to explain His relations to man would at once cause disagreement. There is no definite religious teaching or worship, however meagre, that would claim universal assent.

This admission in no way affects the argument, except by removing a possible misunderstanding as to what we mean by the human experience to which we appeal. We are not rendered doubtful of the fact that all men are mortal, because some African believers in witchcraft refuse their assent. There are multitudes in the race who are unaware that two and two make four. We do not look for our physical knowledge to the universal suffrage of undeveloped minds, but to the furthest researches of cultivated men: and we need not go for religious truth to undeveloped minds, but to the highest experience of pious men. We are not looking vainly for some religious truth that is common to all men, but seeking for the results of the highest spiritual experience of the race. As man's fullest experience of nature is co-ordinated and arranged and described in the body of physical science, so is man's highest religious experience stored and displayed in the Catholic Church: nor is the appeal to this heritage an unreasoning one; as the one body of truth may be verified by scientific men, so may the other by religious men.

It may be asked, however, whether it is not rather arbitrary to decide without discussion that Christianity is the highest embodiment of human religious experience. There are other grand religions—much that is devoted in Islamism, and much that is noble in Buddhism. Why are these to be passed over? And this question cannot be fully answered except by that *Philosophie der Religion*, which shows how the phases of truth which each of these systems contains have been embraced in the completer truth of Christianity. A single suggestion may, however, be thrown out.

There are many people who find a sort of fascination in the comparative study of religions; some who are wholly neglectful of the living power of a faith, are yet curious about different religious systems, as phenomena which may be dissected. Not infrequently this frame of thought results in a double disparagement of Christianity. Hindu stories of incarnations are used to throw discredit on the Christian belief; or moral maxims are quoted which sound as noble, some say nobler than aught in the Gospels. But it is not by picking out parts of a system that religions are to be judged, but by the power of each as a whole. That is the highest religion which *most completely meets the spiritual needs of man*, as none can do unless it tells him of a Father in heaven, reveals the way to that Father, and gives him strength to walk in it. Or to take another form of the test, that is the highest religion which is *most effective in the world;* there is none under the shadow of which such a civilisation has grown as is found in Europe to-day; there is none which is making such successful efforts as those of Christianity to gain a hold on all other regions of the globe.

THE INTERESTS OF CAPITAL AND LABOUR.

PAGE 38.

'THE interests of capital and labour, though apparently conflicting, are in the long-run identical.' This statement has been so often repeated, that there is some danger of its being regarded as a truism which only needs to be stated to meet with approval. But not even apparent truisms should be accepted without some consideration. It is of course clear that some circumstances which are favourable to capital are favourable to labour, *e.g.* a brisk demand, and that often both suffer from the same cause—bad trade; but it does not follow that because they are sometimes similarly affected, that therefore 'their interests are identical.'

Without discussing the question at length, it may suffice to call attention to two cases, in neither of which the interests of the two factors are the same.

It is for the interest of the capitalist that he should be able to take advantage of openings for profitable investment. The greater the fluidity of capital, the more readily it leaves poor speculations and can be transferred into paying concerns, the better for its possessor. With the immense development of limited liability companies, it is more possible than ever before to change capital from one employment to another, or from one country to another; and undoubtedly this tends to the rapid development of the resources of the world and to the profitable employment of capital,—it is for the interest of capitalists. But in what way is it for the interest of the labourers? Labour is not fluid, and cannot readily change from one employment to another or one country to another; and the rapid withdrawal of capital from one employment causes much misery, while the rapid flow of capital into other quarters causes an excessive rise of wages, and produces demoralising results. It may possibly—though I cannot see why—be an advantage to the world at large that this *rapid* development of its resources should go on—rapid improvement of land, rapid development of population, rapid exhaustion of coal; but that is beside the question. We are only concerned to note that while the fluidity of capital is for the interest of capitalists, it is not for the interest of labourers. There is no pretence for saying that it is, unless on the assumption that the new employments of capital always afford such a greatly increased employment for labourers as to make up for all the discomfort connected with emigration, or a change of employment. In some few cases, as, for instance, when railway trains superseded coaches, this has been the case; but there is no proof that it is generally, not to say universally, true. Here, then, is one case where the interests of capitalists and labourers are not identical. It is always the interest of the capitalist to remove his wealth to more profitable employment; it is never for the interest of the labourer that capital should be withdrawn from the avocation he pursues.

To take another case. It is for the interest of the capitalist that his machinery should not stand idle; each hour that is lost renders his fixed capital less remunerative, and therefore shortened hours—especially during daylight—are a serious loss to him, unless accompanied by a reduction of wages that is much greater than proportionate to the reduction of hours. It may be for the interest of the labourer to have shortened hours —Parliament has decreed that it is—and even at the expense of a loss of wages, but it cannot be for his interest to have them shortened and his wages disproportionately reduced. Here there is a possible interest of the labourer's which never can be for the interest of the capitalist.

These facts may cause us to view the apparent truism with distrust; we may look at it more closely. What is meant by *in the long-run?* Does it mean that at some time in the far future, the interests *will be* identical? We cannot point to any period during the last century when they have been so manifestly identical that all strife between the two ceased, and we may discard a truism which turns out to be only a baseless prophecy. Or does it mean *on the average?* Probably this is the case, but then there is a slight absurdity in substituting the more accurate phrase, and saying that the 'interests of capital and labour, though apparently conflicting, are on the average identical.' How can things be identical on an average; and if they are, why do they appear to conflict?

This is not a mere logical quibble; it may even lead us to a better statement of the case. The interests of capital and labour, though always somewhat different, do to a great extent tend in a similar direction; and thus it comes about that though there is a constant dispute between the two, yet on an average, over a period of years, the prosperity of the one is accompanied by the prosperity of the other. But yet the interests are never identical. In good times the capitalist always hopes to drive a better trade without altering his terms with the labourers, the labourer always hopes to get better terms from the capitalist without affecting the conditions of trade. So, too, in bad times, it is for the interest of each that the other should bear the greater share of the loss; but in spite of this constant conflict, it is yet of the highest importance for both that the industry by which both live should not be crippled; and thus on the average, in spite of constant jarring, the main interest of both parties makes itself felt and controls the general course of affairs.

If the interests of capital and labour are thus always distinct, and to some extent different, we need not expect that by giving free play to the self-interest of both classes, we shall obtain a permanent reconciliation; nor can we hope much from the elaborate plans by which men hope to bind the conflicting interests by one yoke, so that they shall always pull together. The system of co-partnerships has not made much progress, because the workman objects—like other people—to putting all his eggs in one basket, and because he is not generally offered any voice in the management of the business. But apart from these things, the system is inherently weak; so long as individual self-interest is to be the motive for industrial conduct, there may arise disputes between the labourers who are not shareholders and those who are; or some men—as in a well-known colliery case—may prefer to be guided by their self-interest as labourers rather than their self-interest as capitalists. So long as these distinct forces have free play, this system will be insufficient to effect a reconciliation.

A bonus on labour is something given as an incitement to more diligent work, and therefore as a means of saving the trouble of superintendence. It may be effective in this way; but this is a mere question of policy in conducting a business, not a case of reconciling rival interests. If, however, there is a real share in the profits given to labourers who have no capital in the business, it must be in either of two ways: (1.) The capitalist is dividing the profits without insisting on the men sharing the risks of the business, and it is against his interest to do so; (2.) The capitalist gives the men a share in the profits, but makes them take a share in the risks, either by actual agreement that they shall do so, or by giving them regular wages at a lowered rate because of the arrangement about bonus. In either case a greater risk connected with the fluctuations of business is thrown on the labourers: irregularity of wage is the greatest evil that can befall the workman, and it is not his interest to adopt this system.

So long as the interests of capital and labour are distinct, and so long as men are supposed to be justified in acting out of mere regard to their own interests, so long is it absurd to consider that any well-meaning system will reconcile the conflicting classes.

In the preceding pages we have pointed out 'a more excellent way' of carrying on our industries; but any readers who desire not merely general principles but practical suggestions, should consult the Rev. C. W. Stubbs' *Village Politics* (Macmillan), the same author's *Glebe Allotments and Co-operative Small Farming* (Allen), and an article on *Communism and Co-operation* in the *Church Quarterly Review* for April 1879.

Edinburgh University Press:
THOMAS AND ARCHIBALD CONSTABLE, PRINTERS TO HER MAJESTY.